why
would
anyone
follow
Jesus?

why would anyone follow Jesus?

12 Reasons to Trust What the Bible Says about Jesus

RAY COMFORT

BakerBooks

a division of Baker Publishing Group
Grand Rapids, Michigan

Published by Baker Books
a division of Baker Publishing Group
PO Box 6287, Grand Rapids, MI 49516-6287
www.bakerbooks.com

Printed in the United States of America

Library of Congress Cataloging-in-Publication Data
Names: Comfort, Ray, author.
Title: Why would anyone follow Jesus? : 12 reasons to trust what the Bible says about Jesus / Ray Comfort.
Description: Grand Rapids, MI : Baker Books, a division of Baker Publishing Group, [2022] | Includes bibliographical references. |
Identifiers: LCCN 2021035429 | ISBN 9781540901774 (paperback) | ISBN 9781540902115 (casebound) | ISBN 9781493433957 (ebook)
Subjects: LCSH: Apologetics. | Jesus Christ.
Classification: LCC BT1103 .C6445 2022 | DDC 239—dc23
LC record available at https://lccn.loc.gov/2021035429

22 23 24 25 26 27 28   7 6 5 4 3 2 1

To my good friend
Tom Hammond

Contents

7

Introduction

There's a particularly heartwarming passage of Scripture in the Gospel of John:

> There were certain Greeks among them that came up to worship at the feast: The same came therefore to Philip, which was of Bethsaida of Galilee, and desired him, saying, Sir, we would see Jesus. (John 12:20–21 KJV)

I have had the honor of preaching in many pulpits, but there is one pulpit I will never forget. Across the top of the surface where I placed my Bible was a small plaque. This plaque faced toward me and any other preacher who used the pulpit. The congregation couldn't see it. It simply said, "Sir, we would see Jesus." That is the cry of every congregation and should be the aim of every preacher. It certainly is my goal with this book—I want you to see Jesus.

When my publisher asked if I would like to write a book that points people to Jesus, I didn't hesitate to say yes. I knew it would be an easy assignment. Writing about my Savior is like talking about my beloved bride. Ask me about Sue, and, if you care to listen, I will spill on you like a burst dam.

I will, with great delight, tell you how we met in a bank in 1967, how she didn't like me at first, how I loved and pursued her, how she changed her mind, and how she eventually proposed. I will explain how she has always been my best friend, how we talk about everything, and how I love to help her do anything. If you care to listen, I will drill a hole through your earlobe, nail it to a door (Exod. 21:5–6; Deut. 15:16–17), and bore you to tears with a thousand stories of the love of my life.

So it is with my precious Savior.

There is no one like my Jesus. He's my greatest love; the light of the world; the hero of heroes; the conqueror of death; the way, the truth, and the life; and the only name under Heaven by which we must be saved. He became my light and lifeline when I was hopelessly sitting in the shadow of death. I'm honored when even one lost person stops and listens to me share His glorious gospel. May the chapters of this book not only help you to see Jesus but also bring you closer to Him.

Ray Comfort

PS: The "Witnessing Encounter" sections at the end of each chapter are transcripts of real-life witnessing encounters captured on video.

1 | Jesus and Intellectual Arguments

Who was Jesus? Was He just a great teacher, or was He the Son of God? Was He the promised Messiah—the one for whom many Jews are still waiting? What if someone told you there is no historical evidence that Jesus even existed? Such a thought removes the wind from the sails of some would-be witnessers. *Live Science* said of Jesus:

> Jesus was the Messiah (Christ), the Son of God who was crucified for the sins of humanity before rising from the dead, according to Christian Gospels and early Christian writings.
>
> According to the Gospels, Jesus, who was born around 4 BC, was able to perform supernatural feats such as healing a wide range of diseases by simply touching people or speaking to them. He supposedly also had the ability to walk on water, instantly create vast amounts of fish and bread, resurrect the dead, rise from the dead himself, calm storms and exorcise demons from people.
>
> The stories told about him have led many scholars to explore these questions: What was Jesus really like? Did he really exist? Today, many of the supernatural feats Jesus is reported to have performed are regarded by scientists as impossible to do—certainly by someone who lived 2,000 years ago.[1]

This article confirms that some *scientists* think that the supernatural feats Jesus did are impossible. What a strange thing to say. *Anyone* can tell you that those feats are impossible to do—today or two thousand years ago when He did them. It's not possible to walk on water, to calm an angry storm just by telling it to, to multiply loaves and fish, or to raise the dead by speaking to them. But the Bible doesn't say only that He did the impossible but also that He *said* things in the same category. His words were seemingly senseless. They were more than wildly strange; they were without precedent—and we will look at many examples in this book.

When someone asks me for evidence that Jesus existed, I ask them a couple of questions. "We mark our yearly time through a numbering system. What number are we up to at present?" When they tell me what year it is, I then ask, "Since when?" The answer is *"since Christ."* We mark the years with the BC/AD dating system. The birth of Jesus is the dividing point of history. No other historical figure so impacted humanity that they were given the honor of splitting time in two. Only Jesus. Napoleon, Shakespeare, Caesar, and Joan of Arc were not given that distinction as a birthmark. Yet no one seriously doubts *their* existence.

We also have the historical records of the four Gospels—Matthew, Mark, Luke, and John. These give us four detailed accounts of Jesus's birth, life, death, and resurrection.

And then there's the record of respected historians. An article on History.com recounts, "The first-century Jewish historian Flavius Josephus . . . twice mentions Jesus in *Jewish Antiquities*, his massive 20-volume history of the Jewish people that was written around AD 93. . . . In one passage of *Jewish Antiquities* that recounts an unlawful execution, Josephus identifies the victim, James, as the 'brother of Jesus-who-is-called-Messiah.'"[2]

The same article describes more evidence, saying the following:

Another account of Jesus appears in *Annals of Imperial Rome*, a first-century history of the Roman Empire written around 116

A.D. by the Roman senator and historian Tacitus. In chronicling the burning of Rome in 64 A.D., Tacitus mentions that Emperor Nero falsely blamed "the persons commonly called Christians, who were hated for their enormities. Christus, the founder of the name, was put to death by Pontius Pilate, procurator of Judea in the reign of Tiberius."[3]

In minutes, we can gather more evidence that Jesus of Nazareth existed than we can of many other historical figures, famous though they may be. Faced with this evidence of His existence, people often start looking around wildly for a detour away from Him. They bring up facts about His life that seem impossible. And one of those pieces of evidence would be His famous words.

Jesus predicted that the heavens and the earth would pass away but that His words would certainly remain (see Matt. 24:35). And two thousand years later, they remain—encapsulated for us in the bestselling book of all time.

No philosopher or historical figure holds a blown-out candle to the brilliance of the words given to us in the Sermon on the Mount. If Jesus didn't give us the Golden Rule and the many other breathtaking truths in that sermon, who did? And why would anyone not want it to be the person whom these detailed historical records maintain it was? One answer to that question is the biblical one. Jesus was hated because He continually spoke of our moral accountability to God: "The world cannot hate you, but it hates Me because I testify of it that its works are evil" (John 7:7).

And that's why He is the only figure in history who has been so despised that His name is used as a popular cuss word.

The Virgin Birth Problem

One popular impossibility that sits forever in the doubter's head and causes many arguments is the virgin birth. The teaching of the

13

Bible is that Jesus was born of a virgin *because* He came to suffer as a sacrificial Lamb for the sin of the world. The Lamb of God had to be without spot or blemish, so Jesus had to be sinless. If He had been born through the lineage of Adam, He would have inherited sin and had tainted blood. Therefore, Joseph couldn't be His father. Jesus's blood had to be pure. Because God was His Father, He had untainted blood.

That's the *why*. I've given the *natural* explanation. Then there's the *supernatural* explanation, the *how*. If we can't accept the virgin birth because we are having a problem with God's abilities, we need to expand our perspective of His power.

Take for example the human body. Scientists estimate it's made up of seventy trillion cells, and each cell contains approximately one hundred trillion atoms. If we want to find out how many atoms make up our bodies, we would multiply seventy trillion by one hundred trillion. Here's my point. God put in order every one of those atoms to make me who I am, and He's intimately familiar with each atom—from the inside out—because He made it. Having knowledge like that can help us refine our understanding of God's power, and from there, expand our thoughts of the immensity of His power. God's power isn't bound by the possible. It reaches into the realm of the impossible.

When religious leaders came to Jesus with a far-fetched scenario in an attempt to confound Him, Jesus pointed to two errors.

> The same day the Sadducees, who say there is no resurrection, came to Him and asked Him, saying: "Teacher, Moses said that if a man dies, having no children, his brother shall marry his wife and raise up offspring for his brother. Now there were with us seven brothers. The first died after he had married, and having no offspring, left his wife to his brother. Likewise the second also, and the third, even to the seventh. Last of all the woman died also. Therefore, in the resurrection, whose wife of the seven will she be? For they all had her."

Jesus answered and said to them, "You are mistaken, not knowing the Scriptures nor the power of God. For in the resurrection they neither marry nor are given in marriage, but are like angels of God in heaven. But concerning the resurrection of the dead, have you not read what was spoken to you by God, saying, 'I am the God of Abraham, the God of Isaac, and the God of Jacob'? God is not the God of the dead, but of the living." And when the multitudes heard this, they were astonished at His teaching. (Matt. 22:23–33)

Jesus told them they were mistaken in two ways: one, they didn't know the Scriptures, and two, they didn't know anything about the power of God. In reality, there are no limits to the power of our Creator. If we adopt the biblical view and give Him *unlimited* power, then we can sit back, relax, and say, "With God nothing will be impossible" (Luke 1:37). This understanding of His power opens the door of reasoning to the virgin birth, the calming of storms, the multiplying of loaves and fish, and the raising of the dead by simply speaking to them.

The Easier Way

But what if you want to do more than simply convince someone that Jesus was born of a virgin? If you want to bring them to Jesus, there's an easier way. If they say, "I *can't* accept the virgin birth," and we try to address that stubborn denial of the biblical account, we are attempting to climb a mountain we need not climb. They're scrambling for a detour, and we need to lead them straight back to Him.

Romans 8:7 says that the carnal mind is in a state of enmity toward God, and that "it is not subject *to the law of God*, nor indeed can be" (emphasis added). In other words, all unregenerate human beings are offended by the moral government of God. This is epitomized in the fact that they use His name in vain. They would never think of using their mother's name as

15

a cuss word, but they use the holy name of the God who gave them life in the place of a filthy word to express disgust. They despise God:

> He who walks in his uprightness fears the LORD,
> But he who is perverse in his ways despises Him.
> (Prov. 14:2)

It is *that* hard ground upon which we sow. And more often than not, the problem is not that they don't understand the concept of the virgin birth; it's that they simply refuse to accept it as truth. Their stumbling block is the sin of unbelief, similar to the unbelief that Zacharias had when the angel of God told him that his elderly wife was going to become pregnant well after she had passed the age of childbearing.

> And Zacharias said to the angel, "How shall I know this? For I am an old man, and my wife is well advanced in years."
> And the angel answered and said to him, "I am Gabriel, who stands in the presence of God, and was sent to speak to you and bring you these glad tidings. But behold, you will be mute and not able to speak until the day these things take place, because you did not believe my words which will be fulfilled in their own time."
> (Luke 1:18–20)

Zacharias was rightly struck dumb because he insulted the integrity of God. It's common for unbelievers to say something like "I find it hard to have faith in God." The question to ask such a person is, "Do you find it hard to have faith in your mother? If so, what does that say about her? It says that she's not trustworthy—that she's a devious liar and not worth trusting."

If it's an insult to someone to lack faith in them, how much more is it an insult to a holy God to lack faith in Him? It is to call him a liar. That's exactly what the Bible says: "He who believes in the Son of God has the witness in himself; he who does not believe God has made Him a liar, because he has not believed the testimony that God has given of His Son" (1 John 5:10).

If our agenda is to convince someone that with God the impossible is possible, we can possibly do that by reasoning about the details of His infinite power. But again, if it's to bring sinners to the Savior, there is an easier way. We simply do what Jesus did. The problem isn't that the virgin birth is a stumbling block in their minds but that their sin is an offense to God. To address an intellectual problem and not the problem of sin is to put the cart before the horse. Or to put it in modern vernacular, we are putting the trailer before the SUV. When we do that, we're not going anywhere.

When the Pharisees wanted a sign from Jesus, He could have pointed to the virgin birth, which Scripture says was a *sign*. The prophet Isaiah foretold: "Therefore the Lord Himself *will give you a sign*: Behold, the virgin shall conceive and bear a Son, and shall call His name Immanuel" (Isa. 7:14, emphasis added).

But Jesus didn't point to the virgin birth. This is what He said instead:

> An evil and adulterous generation seeks after a sign, *and no sign will be given to it except the sign of the prophet Jonah.* For as Jonah was three days and three nights in the belly of the great fish, so will the Son of Man be three days and three nights in the heart of the earth. (Matt. 12:39–40, emphasis added)

Jesus was alluding to the cross—that He would be swallowed by death itself and then be raised back to life. That's the *sign* sinners need. It is the gospel that brings us to God. The gospel—not perfect explanations of supernatural phenomena.

Here's the problem with addressing the human intellect. If somebody is talked into their faith through an intellectual argument, all it will take is a better intellectual argument to talk them out of their faith. However, when the new birth comes to an unbeliever, the moment someone truly believes, they are transformed into a new person (see 2 Cor. 5:17). God takes His law and writes it on the new believer's heart, causing them to walk in His statutes. In other words, the new birth described in John 3 will cause a person to love the things that God loves. I once loved the darkness and hated the light. I once drank iniquity like water. But at the moment of my conversion, I suddenly began to thirst after righteousness. And that's a personal and undeniable miracle for a sin-loving sinner. It was the sign that can never be taken away by a mere argument from a skeptic. When that transformation occurs, we experientially know that with God nothing is impossible, including the virgin birth.

Witnessing Encounter

Fifteen minutes before this interview, I felt inordinately tired. Suspiciously tired. I just wanted to doze off, but I thought, *This is just so obvious; I've got a divine encounter somewhere.* So I stood myself up, went out, found Clarence, and did the following interview—which I'll never forget. Clarence said he was a Christian, that he'd been born again. He said all the right things, but something wasn't right in his heart. I wasn't convinced that he'd truly been born again. I kept that thought in mind throughout the interview, hoping that he wouldn't be offended. He wasn't. After our talk, as Clarence walked away, he said, "Right on time, Ray. . . . Awesome."

    RAY: You say you like information?
    CLARENCE: Yes, I do.
    RAY: Tell me, why is that?
    CLARENCE: Because you can never have too much
       information.

RAY: That's true. There's a Bible verse that says "My people are destroyed for lack of knowledge."[4] There's a lack of information. Have you heard that verse?

CLARENCE: Yes, I have.

RAY: What's the world's biggest selling book of all time?

CLARENCE: The Bible.

RAY: That's the most loved book in the world; it's also the most hated. Why do you think the Bible is hated?

CLARENCE: Because it opens up the truth about each individual. It separates also. It separates because most people want to have their own will and free will to do the things that they want to do, and not God's. And so it separates.

RAY: Have you heard of the Dunning-Kruger effect?

CLARENCE: No, I haven't.

RAY: Two psychologists back in 1999 did a study and found that incompetent people always thought they were competent. That means they thought they could jump higher, run faster, and sing better than what they actually could. All of us are subject to that. I remember back when I was about 13 years old, I thought I could sing pretty good, and I sang into a tape recorder and I played it back and I was horrified at how bad it was. And so for the last 50-something years, if I sing in public, it's always very, very quiet, because I can't sing. Tears come to people's eyes when I start singing. They request that I sing on a hill far away. So now let's see if the Kruger effect goes over to the moral aspect: Clarence, do you think you're a good person?

CLARENCE: A great person.

RAY: I mean morally, are you a good person?

CLARENCE: Morally, a great person.

RAY: So, you're going to do good on judgment day?

CLARENCE: Yes, I am.

RAY: So, there's nothing you're doing or nothing you've done that could offend God or anger Him?

CLARENCE: No, there's nothing to anger God but not following Him and only Him.

RAY: Have you been born again?

CLARENCE: Yes, I have.

RAY: And what does that mean?

CLARENCE: That means to renew your mind and it means to put away the old things and to renew your mind, body, and soul.

RAY: So out of 1 to 10 where would you say you are in your Christian walk? One is really, really bad; 10 is really good.

CLARENCE: I'd say a 7.

RAY: A 7?

CLARENCE: Yeah, 7.

RAY: Now, does that concern you at all?

CLARENCE: Yeah, it always does.

RAY: Yeah, because if I was going to jump out of a plane and you say, "Parachute on tight: 1 to 10" and I said "7," you'd say, "Hey, don't jump on a 7. You want to jump on a 10!" We're talking about your eternity, so we want to make your calling and election sure. So I'm going to see if I can dismantle the fact that you think you're a good person. Do you think I could change your mind?

CLARENCE: No.

RAY: OK. I'm going to use two weapons to shoot it down. Number one I think will work anyway. In Mark 10:18 Jesus says there's none good but God. Who's lying, you or God?

CLARENCE: Me.

RAY: Yes, there's none good. The Bible makes it very clear, and that's because of the fact that *good* in God's book, *good* means "moral excellence." In the dictionary there's over 40 different definitions of the word *good*, and number one is moral excellence—and none of us are good in God's book. When you got up this morning, did you look in the mirror?

CLARENCE: Yes, I did.

RAY: Why did you do that?

CLARENCE: Because I wanted to see my face.

RAY: Yeah, you want to clean up before you go public! You know, puffy eyes, messy hair, whatever. The mirror reveals what you are in truth; it doesn't lie to you. Then it sends you to the water to have a wash. So I'm going to turn the mirror on you so you can see yourself in truth. This will put your Christian walk on steroids, so let's do that. This is the moral law, the Ten Commandments: How many lies do you think you've told in your life?

CLARENCE: I'm not a big liar, but short fibs, I guess. I don't know; I can't really name, little ones here and there.

RAY: Just little lies?

CLARENCE: Yeah.

RAY: What do you call someone who tells lies?

CLARENCE: Untruthful person.

RAY: A liar.

CLARENCE: A liar.

RAY: So what are you?

CLARENCE: I am a truthful person.

RAY: Yeah, but if you tell lies what are you called?

CLARENCE: [laughs]

RAY: Rhymes with fire and begins with *L*. You know, Clarence, it's really hard to judge ourselves.

CLARENCE: A liar.

RAY: Yes, that's it. Now if I told lies, you'd have no trouble saying, "You're a liar." Have you ever stolen something in your whole life, even if it's small?

CLARENCE: Yeah.

RAY: What do you call someone who steals things?

CLARENCE: A thief.

RAY: So what are you?

CLARENCE: A thief.

RAY: No, a lying thief. Do you still think you're a good person?

CLARENCE: Yes, I am.

RAY: You think a lying thief is a good person?

CLARENCE: Yes, he is.

RAY: [laughs] No, he's not.

CLARENCE: Lying thief; it puts you down on number five out of ten, yeah.

RAY: So have you ever used God's name in vain?

CLARENCE: Yes, I have.

RAY: It's using God's name as a cuss word when the Bible says His name is holy. Would you use your mother's name as a cuss word?

CLARENCE: No.

RAY: Because you'll dishonor her, you'll insult her. You'd even anger her, you know, and we anger God when we use His name as a cuss word to express disgust.

CLARENCE: Totally.

RAY: It's called blasphemy and is punishable by death in the Old Testament. Jesus said if you look at a woman and lust for her, you commit adultery with her in your heart. Have you ever looked at a woman with lust?

CLARENCE: Yes.

RAY: Have you had sex before marriage?

CLARENCE: Yes.

RAY: So, Clarence, here's a quick summation. I'm not judging you.

CLARENCE: Break it down.

RAY: Yeah, I'm breaking it down—you've just told me you're a lying, thieving, fornicating, blasphemous adulterer at heart, and you have to face God on judgment day. So if He judges you by the Ten Commandments on judgment day, do you think you'll be innocent or guilty?

CLARENCE: Guilty.

RAY: Heaven or hell?

CLARENCE: I don't want to say that one.

RAY: Well, I will because I love you, I care about you, and if I see you in . . .

CLARENCE: I'm going down.

RAY: Yeah. Say that again?

CLARENCE: I'd go to hell.

RAY: Now does that concern you?

CLARENCE: Very much so.

RAY: Now if you were on a thousand-foot cliff with your toes over the edge, we're talking a thousand-foot cliff, would that be scary for you?

CLARENCE: Yes, surely it would.

RAY: Would the feeling of fear be a horrible feeling?

CLARENCE: Surely it would.

RAY: Is the feeling of fear a good thing or a bad thing?

CLARENCE: Very bad.

RAY: No, it's actually very good—do you know why? Because it's saying, "Step back from the thousand-foot cliff! Don't die! Step back, step back!" So that fear is not your enemy, it's your friend. That's making you step back from that cliff, and what I've tried to do is put you on the edge of eternity and let the fear of God fill your heart, because "the fear of the LORD is the beginning of wisdom."[5] The Scriptures say, "It is a fearful thing to fall into the hands of the living God."[6] Jesus said, "Fear not him who has power to kill your body and afterwards do no more, but fear Him who has power to kill your body and cast your soul into hell."[7] That's a strange thing for Him to say. I don't know if you heard what He just said, but let me say it again. He said, "Fear not him who has power to kill your body."[8] Imagine lying in bed at night; you hear the door creak open in the darkness and you see a guy coming at you with a mask on, with a glittering knife. He pulls the knife back to stab it in your chest! Man, your heart would be in your mouth; you'd be so horrified. But Jesus said, "Don't be afraid of him compared to the fear you should have for God," and so the Bible says, "By the fear of the LORD men depart from evil."[9] And so that fear that I'm trying to put in your heart by God's grace is your friend not your enemy—because it'll make you let go of those beloved sins. We love to fornicate; we love to look at pornography; we even love to lie and steal because, well, it gives us a bit of a buzz. When I was a kid, I used to steal apples from the neighbors. It was more exciting than getting them off the kitchen table!

CLARENCE: I used to take liquor. [laughs]

RAY: You used to take liquor because we've got a sinful heart that loves darkness more than light. So, Clarence, tell me what did God do for guilty sinners so we wouldn't have to go to hell?

CLARENCE: He gave His only begotten Son, so that we should have eternal life.

24

RAY: Yeah, the Bible says the Ten Commandments are called the moral law.

CLARENCE: John 3:15.

RAY: John 3:16. Yeah, you and I broke the law; Jesus paid the fine. That's what happened on that cross. You know, we tend to trivialize sin and say, "It was just white lies and fibs," but the Bible says, "Lying lips *are* an abomination to the LORD."[10] We say we just take little things like candy from a store, but the Bible says thieves will not inherit the kingdom of God, and the way to see how serious God is about sinners is to look at the punishment He's given. Death . . . "the wages of sin is death."[11] Death is evidence that God is deadly serious about sin.

So the fear of God should fill our hearts. Death should make us think, *Man, I don't want to fall into the hands of the living God.* That's a terrifying thing. So Jesus suffered and died on the cross for our sins, took our punishment. If you're in court, Clarence, and someone pays your fine, the judge can legally let you go. He can say, "Clarence, there's a stack of speeding fines here—this is very serious; but someone's paid them, you're free to go," and he can do that which is just and right and legal.

CLARENCE: Right.

RAY: Well, God can legally dismiss our case, forgive our sins, commute our death sentence, actually, take the death sentence off us because Jesus paid the fine on our behalf, rose again on the third day, and defeated death. And now what you have to do, and this is probably what was missing before, is repent of your sins. Now let me explain why I think there's probably a problem. If I said to you, "Clarence, I've got some great news for you, someone just paid a speeding fine on your behalf," but you didn't believe you broke the law, that good news of me paying the fine for you wouldn't be good news; it'd be insulting. You'd say, "What are you talking about? I don't have a speeding fine!" But if you realize you've broken the law—that you went like 60 miles an hour through an area set aside for a blind children's convention, that you did a terrible thing— and I say, "Someone has paid that fine for you," then that good news becomes good news indeed.

So the good news depends on how serious you see your transgression is; and if you see sin as being deadly serious—lying, stealing, using God's name as a cuss word, lusting after women, committing adultery in your heart— then the good news of the cross will make sense to you. You'll find a place of genuine sorrow (and the Bible says, "Godly sorrow produces repentance"[12]), and you'll be able to truly repent, let go of those sins because of the godly sorrow.

That's the first thing; the second thing you must do to be saved is trust in Jesus like you trust a parachute. You don't just *believe* in a parachute; you put your faith into it, and when you have your faith in a parachute, you lose your fear. If you were going to jump 10,000 feet without a parachute, you'd be terrified. But someone gives you a parachute and you trust the parachute; you say, "Oh, I'm safe, I'm going to land at 5 miles an hour on my feet in-stead of 120 miles an hour on my face." When I face death (and it can come at any time), I've got no fear according to the faith I have in Christ. I've put on the Lord Jesus Christ so I can look death in the face. I can look at judgment day and have boldness because I'm trusting in the Savior. I'm trusting in His righteousness. Does this make sense?

CLARENCE: Yes, it does.

RAY: So, Clarence, if you died today and God gave you jus-tice, despite your intellectual belief and knowing so much truth, you'd end up in hell. There are two things you must do to be saved—you must repent and trust alone in Jesus. When are you going to do that?

CLARENCE: I've already done it.

RAY: Yes, but remember the fruit wasn't there, so I think you should do it again.

CLARENCE: [immediately begins to pray] Dear God, I ask You right now to come into my heart and renew my mind. I ask You to work on my dailies, my thoughts, my endeavors, and everything that's in front of me. Let Your will be done and not mine. All these things I ask in the mighty name of Christ. Amen.

RAY: I pray for Clarence that today he'll see sin in a different light and find a place of godly sorrow and bring forth fruit worthy of repentance and know that he's passed from death to life. And that his walk will be one of holiness and glorifying You, and may You raise him up as a burning and a shining light to reach this generation, in Jesus's name we pray.

CLARENCE: Amen.

RAY: Amen, amen.

CLARENCE: Amen.

God can do the impossible—He can break through the lies that people like Clarence tell themselves all the time. After all, the lie "I'm a good person" is easier for most people than the truth of the virgin birth!

Special note: I'm often asked why I don't "close the deal" with the lost by having them pray what is commonly called the sinner's prayer. Think of Nathan and King David (see 2 Sam. 12). When David's sin was exposed, Nathan didn't say, "Pray this prayer after me and mean it from your heart." Instead, he stood back and let the Lord work in David's heart. David sought the Lord himself and prayed the penitent prayer of Psalm 51 from his own conviction.

When I was a new Christian, I found a popular little booklet that laid out the gospel as four laws. I didn't notice at the time that it didn't open up the Ten Commandments for the reader as Jesus did for His audience. Nor did it mention hell or hint of judgment day. This little booklet held up Jesus as a means of happiness. It didn't mention that Jesus is the One who gives us the righteousness we need to be saved from God's wrath. In my ignorance, I led twenty-eight of my surfing buddies to Jesus. I'd give them the four laws and then have them repeat the sinner's prayer at the end. It was so easy and simple. The trouble was, twenty-seven of the twenty-eight tragically backslid and became bitter against God. If we water down the medicine, it will lose its curative properties.

It's worth noting that my friends who backslid didn't actually backslide. They never slid forward in the first place. They had false conversions, and I was responsible. God forgive me. There's a much more effective way to evangelize. This way leaves out the sinner's prayer, but it gives God all the room in the world to work in sinners' hearts. Think of what happened after the Ethiopian eunuch was saved (see Acts 8:26–40). He was left without follow-up. The Spirit of God transported Philip the evangelist away and left the new convert alone in the wilderness. Perhaps this story is in Scripture to remind us that the new convert's salvation wasn't dependent on Philip but on his relationship with God. If God is the author of someone's faith, He will be the finisher (see Heb. 12:2). If God has begun a good work in us, He will complete it (see Phil. 1:6). He is able to keep each of us from falling and present us faultless before the presence of His glory with exceeding joy (see Jude 1:24).

I do pray with and for penitent sinners. Then I give them our booklet called *The Bible's Four Gospels*.[13] This booklet was produced especially for new converts and those who are open to the things of God. It contains the four Gospels, the twenty most commonly asked questions of the Christian faith, and the text of our very popular booklet *Why Christianity?* After I give them this publication, I commend them into the hands of the faithful Creator.

2 | Jesus and Hope

The Sermon on the Mount is without question the greatest sermon ever preached—delivered by the greatest preacher who ever lived and recorded in the greatest book ever written. It's called the Sermon on the Mount because it was preached on a mountain. It is an unchallenged Everest, high above any other words uttered by mortal lips. Nothing comes even remotely close. The Sermon on the Mount, found in Matthew 5–7, is a call to hope that rings throughout the ages, even all the way to the present.

The opening verse to this most marvelous sermon pulls back the curtains and tells us what it was that Jesus looked upon before He climbed the mount. Scripture says in the first verse of the sermon, "And *seeing* the multitudes" (Matt. 5:1, emphasis added). The sight of so many human beings likely influenced His decision to make the climb. Perhaps the multitude had thronged Him, and He wanted to get away because He had some special words that were just for His disciples. Or perhaps Jesus was wanting His disciples to look down on the multitude and get a different perspective. Sometimes it's only when we get above a situation that we can see it clearly.

For some reason, the crowd didn't follow Jesus. It seems that this sermon (though universal to all humankind through the Scriptures) was for the privileged ears of the disciples, as we are told, "when He was seated *His disciples* came to Him" (v. 1, emphasis added). Jesus needed to tell them a thing or two about hope. Judas was one of those privileged hearers. He was there to hear the greatest sermon ever preached, yet it didn't sink down into his heart. He was numbered with the disciples, yet time would prove him to be a traitor. Such thoughts should make us shudder. We must ask ourselves if a seed of betrayal could ever find root in our own hearts. Would we climb a hill to be with Jesus, hear His gracious words, and yet betray Him with a kiss because we secretly loved sin? One of the greatest favors we can ever do for ourselves is to pray the following:

> Search me, O God, and know my heart;
> Try me, and know my anxieties;
> And see if there is any wicked way in me,
> And lead me in the way everlasting. (Ps. 139:23–24)

Judas was a disciple, but he wasn't a disciple "indeed" (see John 8:31–32). He was a first-class hope resister. Deeds speak louder than words. Those who truly believe don't just follow Jesus; they obey Him from the heart. They follow Him up a hill, sit at His feet, and *learn* from Him. They learn to hope the way He teaches them to hope. When Jesus washed His disciples' feet, He made a subtle reference to Judas: "Jesus said to him, 'He who is bathed needs only to wash his feet, but is completely clean; and you are clean, but not all of you.' For He knew who would betray Him; therefore He said, 'You are not all clean'" (John 13:10–11).

Judas is one of my favorite Bible characters. He is a signpost of where I should never go. His short life tells me to beware of a hidden covetousness. He heard Jesus say, "You are not all clean," but he didn't purify his heart. Even when Jesus said, "Assuredly, I say to you, one of you will betray Me" (Matt. 26:21), he didn't come clean. He harbored sin in his heart right until the moment that Satan entered him (see Luke 22:3). Judas gives me all kinds of reasons to place my hope in Jesus because I don't want to be anything like him.

Earlier in the book of John, we are told that Jesus knew who believed (see 6:64). He had tested their commitment to Him by speaking very objectionable words about eating His flesh and drinking His blood (see vv. 48–58). But it is clear that He wasn't speaking of a literal eating of flesh and drinking of blood. He said the same thing at the Passover when He instituted communion for believers: "And as they were eating, Jesus took bread, blessed and broke it, and gave it to the disciples and said, 'Take, eat; this is My body'" (Matt. 26:26).

Jesus wasn't referring to the disgusting practice of cannibalism. It is obvious that the bread wasn't His literal body because He was standing there with them. It was *symbolic*. His words were spiritual. He said, "It is the Spirit who gives life; the flesh profits nothing. The words that I speak to you are spirit, and they are life" (John 6:63). It is when we are born of the Spirit (see John 3:1–3) that we are able to "taste and see that the LORD is good" (Ps. 34:8). Still, the natural mind instantly recoils at such words, and that was the case with His superficial hearers: "Therefore many of His disciples, when they heard this, said, 'This is a hard saying; who can understand it?'" (John 6:60), and many of them turned back from following Him (see v. 66).

Look at what Jesus then said and how Peter reacted to His words:

When Jesus knew in Himself that His disciples complained about this, He said to them, "Does this offend you? What then if you should see the Son of Man ascend where He was before? It is the Spirit who gives life; the flesh profits nothing. The words that I speak to you are spirit, and they are life. But there are some of you who do not believe." For Jesus knew from the beginning who they were who did not believe, and who would betray Him. And He said, "Therefore I have said to you that no one can come to Me unless it has been granted to him by My Father."

From that time many of His disciples went back and walked
with Him no more. Then Jesus said to the twelve, "Do you also
want to go away?"

But Simon Peter answered Him, "Lord, to whom shall we go?
You have the words of eternal life. Also we have come to believe
and know that You are the Christ, the Son of the living God."
(John 6:61–69)

To whom can we go when we don't understand the hard sayings
of Scripture or when we go through fiery trials? There's no one
but Jesus who can take us through this life and into the next. In
Him alone we have hope. But that can only come to us if we are
trusting in the risen Savior, not in an unbiblical belief that Jesus is
literal bread. Through the new birth we have a *living* hope in our
death that is based on the immutable promises of God. And that
gives meaning and purpose to life. The famous song "American
Pie" asks the most relevant of questions: "Did you write the book
of love and do you have faith in God above?" And then it speaks
of the Bible and asks if you believe in rock 'n' roll and if music
can save your soul.

For years fans have wondered at the meaning of other parts of
the song. Late in 2020, an aging Don McLean was interviewed
about what he was going through when he penned the pie:

When Don McClean was 15 years old, his father dropped dead
right in front of him. . . .

The singer-songwriter behind the 1971 classic American Pie is
speaking from his home in Palm Desert, a town in California where
he is now well into what he calls the "desert phase" of his life.
Wildfires are still burning across the state. You can't see the sun for
the acrid smoke. "I'm feeling it in my lungs," says the 75-year-old.

So what did he do when his father died? "I cried for two years,"
he says. "I blamed myself." We've been talking about death for half
an hour—his father's and his feelings about his own. "I'm nearing the end of the high-dive," he says. "Know what I mean?" . . .

34

But then there's no point asking McLean direct questions about what the song means: he's too well practised at flicking them off. "It means I'll never have to work again," he used to quip.[1]

When any of us are nearing the end of the "high-dive," it is wise to know if we will be hitting water or rock. When we go off the high-dive, in what are we placing our hope?

Is the ultimate goal in life to work at being so rich that we never have to work again? Most enjoy work, and coming home after a hard day's work is pleasant. It's workdays that tend to make weekends enjoyable.

"All work and no play makes Jack a dull boy" is a well-used proverb. It means that "without time off from work, a person becomes both bored and boring."[2] But no work makes Jack a depressed boy, and according to the CDC, in June of 2020, when unemployment was high, nearly 11 percent of Americans seriously considered committing suicide.[3]

Without a living hope in God, life lacks purpose, and that is depressingly deadly. Jesus warned what would happen to those who ignored His words:

> Therefore whoever hears these sayings of Mine, and does them, I will liken him to a wise man who built his house on the rock: and the rain descended, the floods came, and the winds blew and beat on that house; and it did not fall, for it was founded on the rock.
>
> But everyone who hears these sayings of Mine, and does not do them, will be like a foolish man who built his house on the sand: and the rain descended, the floods came, and the winds blew and beat on that house; and it fell. And great was its fall. (Matt. 7:24–27)

Witnessing Encounter

Jennifer looked like she was in her early twenties. She sat alone outdoors at a local college. As you'll see, she was sorely in need of some hope. When I approached her and asked if she thought there was an afterlife, she said she did. Then she kindly agreed to come on camera.

RAY: Do you think there's an afterlife?

JENNIFER: I believe there's an afterlife, and I think I made this assumption based more on hope that, in all the tragedies that I face now, there might be something better for me in the afterlife.

RAY: There's got to be something better than this.

JENNIFER: Yeah, of course.

RAY: Disease, pain, suffering, and death. There is nothing good on the news. A lot of people committing suicide. Life is depressing. Let me ask you something. Do you ever think about your brain?

JENNIFER: Actually, no.

RAY: Don't you think how incredible it is? It's four inches of sponge; if you threw it to a dog, it would probably eat it. And yet it contains so much information—it's processing my voice at the moment through your ears into your brain. It's processing what you see with your eyes. It's processing your emotions, everything you've got, everything you're feeling is going through that brain. And all the computers in the world combined can't do what the dumbest human brain can do. Do you ever think about that?

JENNIFER: Actually, yes.

RAY: Do you ever think about the One that made the brain?

JENNIFER: Wow, that's new. My brain has never got that curious.

RAY: Have you ever thought about how incredible God is to create the brain? Or are you an atheist?

JENNIFER: Oh, no, I believe in God. And, yes, I would say that I think God created the brain. It makes me think this way. Based on His creation, I see how more powerful He is.

RAY: Do you ever thank God that you can think? I mean, one fall onto concrete from five feet, a bang on the brain, and your eyes would be nothing. Hearing would mean nothing. All your emotions, all your memories would go with a bang on the head if you damage that brain. Do you ever thank God for your thoughts? For your eyesight? For your life? Do you ever look at the sky and say, "Thank You, Lord, for Your creation"? Or not.

JENNIFER: Oh, yes. I was severely depressed a couple of weeks ago . . . still kind of working through it now. And one thing that made my mornings and my day go much better, every day waking up and naming five things that I'm grateful for. The sky being blue, for it to be raining, for breathing, for seeing. And it's just those simple things that every day I thank God for.

RAY: Do you ever get suicidal thoughts?

JENNIFER: You know what? Sometimes.

RAY: When I grabbed my microphone to interview you, I grabbed a little booklet called *How to Battle Depression and Suicidal Thoughts* because I wanted to give it to you. So God knows what you're going through. Now let me ask a very important question. Do you think God is happy with you or angry at you?

JENNIFER: I think God is really happy with me.

RAY: Are you a good person?

JENNIFER: I try to be.

RAY: I'm going to put that to the test. I'm going to try and change your mind, and there's a reason for it. If it's uncomfortable, stay with me, because we're going to come out of the tunnel into the light. How many lies have you told in your life?

JENNIFER: [sighs] Many.

RAY: Have you ever stolen something?

JENNIFER: Oh, no.

RAY: That's not one of those many lies? Have you ever taken anything that belongs to somebody else, even if it's small, irrespective of its value? God as your witness.

JENNIFER: Oh, yeah. I would say sometimes, where there's little candies on a little plate. I don't know if I'm allowed to take one. It's the store's or I mean, or like . . .

RAY: We tend to trivialize theft by saying "just little things." Little stores, little candy, little lady sold it to me, but God takes lying and thieving very seriously. Have you ever used God's name in vain?

JENNIFER: Yes.

RAY: He gave you your life, your eyesight, your hearing. Everything you've got came from God. Would you use your mother's name as a cuss word?

JENNIFER: No.

RAY: Why not?

JENNIFER: Because for me, my mother is one of the precious things I have, and I wouldn't want to disrespect her that way.

RAY: And yet, you have taken the name of God, the holy name of God, and used it as a cuss word to express disgust, which is called "blasphemy," punishable by death in the Old Testament.

JENNIFER: I've underestimated His power, and I've also taken Him for granted. And I'm going to be honest, I know for a fact because I've disrespected His name.

RAY: Jesus said, if you look with lust, you commit adultery in your heart. Have you ever looked with lust?

JENNIFER: Hmm. Yes.

RAY: Have you had sex before marriage?

JENNIFER: Yes.

RAY: So, Jennifer, I'm not judging you (and thanks for your honesty), but you've told me you're a lying, thieving, blasphemous, fornicating adulterer at heart. Do you still think you're a good person?

JENNIFER: Yes.

RAY: That's called "self-righteousness," and it's calling God a liar, because God says there's none good but Him. You know what *good* means? It means to be morally perfect. If you look in the dictionary, there are forty different definitions of the word *good*. Number one is "moral excellence." None of us are good in God's book. None of us are morally excellent. So here's the big question. If God judges you by the Ten Commandments (we've looked at four of them) on judgment day, are you going to be innocent or guilty?

JENNIFER: Guilty.

RAY: Heaven or hell?

JENNIFER: Hell.

RAY: Does that concern you?

JENNIFER: Of course.

RAY: Because you want to live. You don't want to be damned by God. So we're coming out of the tunnel now; it's been dark. What did God do for guilty sinners so you wouldn't have to go to hell? Do you know?

JENNIFER: [silence]

RAY: Well, you actually do, but you've forgotten. Jesus died on the cross for the sin of the world. You and I broke

God's law, the Ten Commandments; Jesus paid the fine. That's what happened on that cross. That's why He said, "It is finished" just before He died. Jennifer, if you're in court and someone pays your fine, a judge can let you go even though you're guilty. The judge can say, "Jennifer, there's a stack of speeding fines here. This is deadly serious. But someone's paid them. You're free to go." And even though you're guilty, he can let you go and do that which is legal and right and just. God has made a way through the death and resurrection of the Savior for Him to let you go, even though you're guilty, and to take the death sentence off you and let you live forever—even though you have a multitude of sins—because He's rich in mercy and He provided a Savior. Jesus paid the fine so you could walk out of the courtroom. And then He rose from the dead and defeated death, your greatest enemy. And, Jennifer, if you'll repent (an old-fashioned word—it means to confess and forsake your sins), if you'll turn from your sins and trust in Jesus, you have God's promise He'll grant you everlasting life as a free gift.

Are you going to think about what we talked about?

JENNIFER: Of course, yes.

RAY: Are you going to *seriously* think about it?

JENNIFER: Yes, because it made me think about how all these things are true. It made me realize how me walking away from my faith and hope from God—because I used to go to church, pray, and thank Him for everything. The minute I started moving away from that, I guess that's when my life became depressed, sad, and I found no motive to continue. When He was my motive.

RAY: You know, Jesus said that if you put your hand on the plow and even look back, you're not fit for the kingdom. So get before the Lord, truly confess and forsake your sins, and trust in Jesus like you trust a parachute, and then pick up a Bible and read it. And as you obey His Word, He promises to reveal Himself to you. In John 14:21 Jesus said, "He that has My commandments and keeps them, it is he that loves Me. And he that loves Me will be loved by My Father, and I will love him and reveal Myself to him."[4] I've got some literature for you, including that little booklet *How to Battle Depression and Suicidal Thoughts*. Thank you.

Witnessing to others about Jesus is primarily why we exist as the church. Jesus said that we are to be *His* witnesses (see Acts 1:8). If they want to tell you about their pain, listen. Then point them to the hope that you have found in Christ, the only true source of hope that can be found anywhere.

3 | Jesus and Money

Jesus of Nazareth gave sight to the blind, healed the sick, raised the dead, and spoke words that were so gracious even His enemies marveled. So it's not surprising that massive crowds wanted to go in person to see if the rumors they had heard about this man were true. Yet among the passages of Scripture that speak of His incredible popularity, there is a strange verse: "And behold, the whole city came out to meet Jesus. And when they saw Him, they begged Him to depart from their region" (Matt. 8:34).

The entire city came to meet Jesus. When they saw Him, they asked Him to leave the area. They didn't suggest that He do so. They *begged* Him to go. Typically, crowds clung to Jesus, but these people were desperate for a detour away from Him. Something very strange led up to the incident:

> When He had come to the other side, to the country of the Gerge-senes, there met Him two demon-possessed men, coming out of the tombs, exceedingly fierce, so that no one could pass that way. And suddenly they cried out, saying, "What have we to do with You, Jesus, You Son of God? Have You come here to torment us before the time?"

Now a good way off from them there was a herd of many swine feeding. So the demons begged Him, saying, "If You cast us out, permit us to go away into the herd of swine."

And He said to them, "Go." So when they had come out, they went into the herd of swine. And suddenly the whole herd of swine ran violently down the steep place into the sea, and perished in the water.

Then those who kept them fled; and they went away into the city and told everything, including what had happened to the demon-possessed men. (Matt. 8:28–33)

The people didn't bring their sick to Jesus to be healed; they didn't come to hear His gracious words. They came because the herders who kept the pigs had fled into the city and told them everything that had occurred, including what had happened to the two demon-possessed men. They had seen demons leave them and cause two thousand screaming pigs to violently run off a cliff and die (see Mark 5:13).

The Gospel of Luke gives us a little more information: "Then the whole multitude of the surrounding region of the Gadarenes asked Him to depart from them, *for they were seized with great fear*" (8:37, emphasis added).

It seems odd that they would be "seized with great fear." The demon-possessed men had been delivered from demons. The whole city should have been rejoicing over the men's freedom, but they weren't. Perhaps they were fearful that Jesus would further ruin their local economy. After all, with one word He had destroyed a lucrative hog business. Maybe the local insurance agent didn't see this as "an act of God" and wouldn't cover the loss. Like the rich young ruler (see the next section), they couldn't see beyond their love of money to something infinitely more precious. John Wesley said, "*They besought him to depart out of their coasts—* They loved their swine so much better than their souls! How many are of the same mind!"[1] This town saw that the love of God and the love of money couldn't go together—and they unanimously chose money!

|||||||||||||

Scripture warns us that "the love of money is a root of all kinds of evil" (1 Tim. 6:10). The horrific evil of abortion—the killing of precious human beings in the womb—is driven by the love of money. Billions of dollars each year pass through bloody hands and line evil pockets. The love of money is the lucrative oil that fuels the sale of illegal drugs. It is the oil that runs the alcohol and gambling industries, prostitution, and many other vices of the world. And those who are given to greed cannot serve both God and money. Jesus said, "No one can serve two masters; for either he will hate the one and love the other, or else he will be loyal to the one and despise the other. You cannot serve God and mammon" (Matt. 6:24).

Like hungry pigs, those greedy for gain think only of feeding their insatiable appetites. They trample the gospel underfoot. Jude didn't mince words in his description of those given to greed:

[They] are spots in your love feasts, while they feast with you without fear, serving only themselves. They are clouds without water, carried about by the winds; late autumn trees without fruit, twice dead, pulled up by the roots; raging waves of the sea, foaming up their own shame; wandering stars for whom is reserved the blackness of darkness forever. (Jude 1:12–13)

Neither did Peter:

But these, like natural brute beasts made to be caught and destroyed, speak evil of the things they do not understand, and will utterly perish in their own corruption, and will receive the wages of unrighteousness, as those who count it pleasure to carouse in the daytime. They are spots and blemishes, carousing in their own deceptions while they feast with you, having eyes full of adultery and that cannot cease from sin, enticing unstable souls. They have a heart trained in covetous practices, and are accursed children. (2 Pet. 2:12–14)

The greedy have a heart *trained* in covetous practices. Because of their greed Jesus is a threat to them, as He was a threat to the covetous, rich young ruler who went away sorrowful.

Now as He was going out on the road, one came running, knelt before Him, and asked Him, "Good Teacher, what shall I do that I may inherit eternal life?"

So Jesus said to him, "Why do you call Me good? No one is good but One, that is, God. You know the commandments: 'Do not commit adultery,' 'Do not murder,' 'Do not steal,' 'Do not bear false witness,' 'Do not defraud,' 'Honor your father and your mother.'"

And he answered and said to Him, "Teacher, all these things I have kept from my youth."

Then Jesus, looking at him, loved him, and said to him, "One thing you lack: Go your way, sell whatever you have and give to the poor, and you will have treasure in heaven; and come, take up the cross, and follow Me."

But he was sad at this word, and went away sorrowful, for he had great possessions. (Mark 10:17–22)

The love of money is a detour that drowns men in destruction and perdition. Greed took hold of Judas and hung him by the neck, and it will suffocate all who give themselves to it. Nothing compares to the treasure we have in earthen vessels—the real treasure, which is our souls. If we gain the whole world and lose our souls, we've lost everything. The poorest of paupers who dies with the riches of Christ is richer than the richest rich person who dies in their sins. The city that chased Jesus away was too afraid to accept that truth. Their love of money only made them fearful, and they headed for the detour.

Fear doesn't just manifest itself in the love of money, however. Someone once asked me why God created demons, and if there was no threat of hell, would people still worship Him? Did He create the demonic realm? If so, why? That opens a can of worms about the integrity of God. There are many more questions that open even more cans. If He's good, why does He allow the evil of satanic abuse? And not only that evil but the evil of Nazi Germany, murder, rape, torture, and a mass of other things? Why do some people have different interpretations of Scripture? And there's the very old question of whether we would love God if there were no hell. That answer delves into the depth of human depravity.

All these difficult questions were plaguing the questioner and causing him to doubt both God's existence and His integrity. Or were they?

There's a better way to address this man's supposed doubt than to run down his rabbit trails. The Bible tells us that he *knows* that God exists (see Rom. 1:20). We are also told that he is held captive to his lust: "But every man is tempted, when he is drawn away of his own lust, and enticed" (James 1:14 KJV).

Not only is he drawn away by his own sin, but he loves it: "And this is the condemnation, that the light has come into the world, and men loved darkness rather than light, because their deeds were evil. For everyone practicing evil hates the light and does not come to the light, lest his deeds should be exposed" (John 3:19–20).

When I responded (in the comments below the video) with one question, "Into porn?" he wrote back, "Sometimes." Experience told me that he didn't want answers. He wanted to hide behind a mountain of questions so that he could secretly indulge in the sin he loved but knew was morally wrong. If God wasn't real, his sin didn't matter. I have been where he is, so it's not difficult for me to follow the admonition of Scripture when speaking with him about his sin: "And a servant of the Lord must not quarrel but be gentle to all, able to teach, patient, in humility correcting those who are in opposition, if God perhaps will grant them repentance, so that they may know the truth, and that they may come to their senses and escape the snare of the devil, having been taken captive by him to do his will" (2 Tim. 2:24–26).

The devil holds him captive, and in serving sin, he is doing the devil's will. His only hope of breaking free is the gospel of Jesus Christ. As sinners, our *real* problem is that we don't want to let go of our sin—our refusal to surrender is much deeper than our interest in complicated questions. That's where the power of the gospel helps us. Look at how Paul described its power: "For I am not ashamed of the gospel of Christ, *for it is the power of God to salvation* for everyone who believes . . ." (Rom. 1:16, emphasis added).

The gospel as "the power of God to salvation" isn't confined to deliverance from death. It also promises deliverance from sin. God not only forgives our sins and saves us from death; He also gives us a new heart that thirsts after righteousness. The entice-ment of sin still exists, but our new heart gives us the power (and the will) to overcome temptation: "No temptation has overtaken you except such as is common to man; but God is faithful, who will not allow you to be tempted beyond what you are able, but with the temptation will also make the way of escape, that you may be able to bear it" (1 Cor. 10:13).

It is because of the gospel that we are no longer enemies of God in our minds through wicked works. He is now *for* us, not against us, and will therefore help us in our temptations, making a way of escape. My friend the commenter needed to see his sins and his consequential terrible danger and embrace the glorious gospel. Jesus is his only hope. Answers to his other questions wouldn't have even touched the real problem in his heart.

We don't see the wicked hearts of those with whom we speak, but God certainly does: "Now the Pharisees, *who were lovers of money*, also heard all these things, and they derided [Jesus]. And He said to them, 'You are those who justify yourselves before men, but God knows your hearts. For what is highly esteemed among men is an abomination in the sight of God'" (Luke 16:14–15, emphasis added).

How, then, do we reach these sin-loving sinners with the gospel? The answer is in what Jesus pointed to in the following verses: "The law and the prophets were until John. Since that time the kingdom of God has been preached, and everyone is pressing into it. And it is easier for heaven and earth to pass away than for one tittle of the law to fail" (vv. 16–17).

Do we understand that Jesus is the answer, or are we desperate for the detour? The answer lies in whether we see our desperate need of the mercy of God. The Bible says of the poor that they heard Jesus gladly (see Mark 12:37). Those who are genuinely poor don't know where their next meal is coming from. They don't have large bank accounts, and so their trust isn't in their money. They usually have humble hearts because the pains of life have humbled them. The rich, however, are sometimes puffed up peacock proud, and because of their wealth they see no need to trust in God because their faith is in their riches. Money supplies their needs. It gives them peace and joy, and it gives them a warm sense of security. Jesus said that it's harder for a rich man to enter Heaven than it is for a camel to go through the eye of a needle (see Matt. 19:24). They're not easy to thread. It seems that these villagers trusted in the wealth provided by the pigs—and that's why they begged Jesus to leave.

However, humility doesn't necessarily mean that we see our need of God's mercy. Dire circumstances may open our ears, but we must see our sin before we see our need of the Savior. A poor man may beg for Jesus to help him financially, but he must also beg Him to save him from the consequences of his sin. Peter only called out to Jesus when he saw his danger of drowning:

49

And Peter answered Him and said, "Lord, if it is You, command me to come to You on the water."

So He said, "Come." And when Peter had come down out of the boat, he walked on the water to go to Jesus. But when he saw that the wind was boisterous, he was afraid; and beginning to sink he cried out, saying, "Lord, save me!" (Matt. 14:28–30)

Danger made Peter desperate. He knew he needed Jesus to save him. The Philippian jailer didn't cry out to be saved until an earthquake put the fear of God in his heart:

At midnight Paul and Silas were praying and singing hymns to God, and the prisoners were listening to them. Suddenly there was a great earthquake, so that the foundations of the prison were shaken; and immediately all the doors were opened and everyone's chains were loosed. And the keeper of the prison, awaking from sleep and seeing the prison doors open, supposing the prisoners had fled, drew his sword and was about to kill himself. But Paul called with a loud voice, saying, "Do yourself no harm, for we are all here."

Then he called for a light, ran in, and fell down trembling before Paul and Silas. And he brought them out and said, "Sirs, what must I do to be saved?" (Acts 16:25–30)

We must learn how to give sinners their own boisterous storm or earthquake to shake them out of their complacency. We must hope that they desperately beg for Jesus to save them—He is the only real answer to the longings in their hearts. We do that with the law of God.

Witnessing Encounter

Again, every unsaved person needs their own personal earthquake to make them look heavenward. And my agenda was to try and gently shake a young man I spoke with in a phone conversation.

I had to buy a new filter for a water dispenser and had a problem doing it online. I called the company that made the dispenser and left a message. The next day, a young man named Adrian called and said that he could help. I told him that I was driving up our driveway, and it would take about thirty seconds to get inside and give him my credit card details.

As I was walking in, I made small talk. He said he was calling from Texas, so I asked how the weather was out there. He said it was gloomy. I told him I lived in Southern California and that we could see what we were breathing. He said, "I know, I've seen it on the news. It looked terrible."

I said that it wasn't as bad as San Francisco—where the whole city was a ghastly orange color because of surrounding forest fires. When he said he had seen San Francisco, I responded, "It's almost apocalyptic."

Adrian answered with a concern in his voice, "Yes, I know. I've been thinking about that."

I then asked if he was a Christian.

He hesitated, then said, "I've been thinking that I need to get back to church."

I said, "Let's order the filter and then I'd like to speak to you for a few minutes about something far more important than a water filter."

Five minutes later, I said, "Let's get back to what we were talking about, very briefly. May I ask you a question?" He said that it was fine.

RAY: Do you think you're a good person?

ADRIAN: Yes, I am.

RAY: How many lies do you think you've told in your life?

ADRIAN: More than I can count. I'm *not* a good person.

RAY: Have you ever stolen anything?

ADRIAN: I don't think so.

He had blasphemed God's name, and when I asked him if he would ever use his mother's name as a cuss word and related it to the fact that he didn't respect or love God, he went very quiet. He said that he had lusted after women and admitted that he would be guilty on judgment day. When I asked if he would go to Heaven or hell, he went *deathly* silent. That's when I jumped in and said that the Bible says that all liars will have their part in the lake of fire, and that no thief, no blasphemer, and no adulterer would enter the kingdom of God.

RAY: So can you see that you're in big trouble?

ADRIAN: Yes.

RAY: Would you go to Heaven or hell?

ADRIAN: But didn't Jesus die for our sins?

RAY: He did, and most people know that. But if you can get a grip on what I'm going to tell you next, it will be life changing.

That's when I told him that we broke God's law, and Jesus paid the fine. I related Jesus's sacrifice to a colossal fine being paid by another. Then I shared about the necessity of repentance and faith in Jesus. I also spoke to him about how fear can be our friend, not our enemy, and that I hoped he had begun to fear God that day because through the fear of the Lord men depart from evil. I quickly gave him our YouTube channel address, saying that if he just typed in "Living Waters" he would find videos to help him grow in his faith. He thanked me sincerely for talking to him and said that it had given him a lot to think about.

I live in an earthquake zone and have often given thought as to where the safest place would be in a big one. My only conclusion has been to be in a helicopter. Unlike planes, they don't need a smooth runway to land safely. But in the ultimate shakeup of judgment day, the only safe place will be in Christ. He is the solid rock upon which we stand, and nothing will shake those who belong to Him.

4 | Jesus and Exclusivity

When Jesus said, "I am the way, the truth, and the life. No one comes to the Father except through Me" (John 14:6), He nullified every other religion's teaching that they lead to God, to the truth, or to Heaven. Jesus was saying it's His way to Heaven or the highway to hell. And this wasn't a slip of the divine tongue. John 14:6 does not give any wiggle room for a translation error. Check out this description from quora.com:

> The Greek text is rather unambiguous and there doesn't seem to be any textual variants in the manuscripts. The standard English translation is almost a literal translation of the Greek:
> λέγει αὐτῷ ὁ Ἰησοῦς· ἐγώ εἰμι ἡ ὁδὸς καὶ ἡ ἀλήθεια καὶ ἡ ζωή· οὐδεὶς ἔρχεται πρὸς τὸν πατέρα εἰ μὴ δι' ἐμοῦ. (John 14:6)
> Jesus said to him, "I am the way and the truth and the life. No one comes to the Father except [literal: if not] through me. (*New American Bible*).[1]

The verse is not an isolated doctrine. There are many other verses like it. Here's a small sampling:

- "Most assuredly, I say to you, I am the door of the sheep. All who ever came before Me are thieves and robbers" (John 10:7–8).

- "The things which the Gentiles sacrifice they sacrifice to demons and not to God, and I do not want you to have fellowship with demons" (1 Cor. 10:20).
- "For there is one God and one Mediator between God and men, the Man Christ Jesus" (1 Tim. 2:5).
- "Whoever transgresses and does not abide in the doctrine of Christ does not have God. He who abides in the doctrine of Christ has both the Father and the Son" (2 John 1:9).

Was Jesus being exclusive? Yes. His exclusivity is paradoxical in that the modern world says such intolerance should not be tolerated. To preach His words is to be a narrow-minded, hateful, antiscience, fundamentalist bigot. But we have no choice. There are many who try to make the words of Jesus more palatable and less exclusive. Those who profess to have faith in Jesus while saying there are many ways to God may have the world's approval for now, but that isn't the approval that matters. Look at what Jesus said about those who compromise His words: "For whoever is ashamed of Me *and My words*, of him the Son of Man will be ashamed when He comes in His own glory, and in His Father's, and of the holy angels" (Luke 9:26, emphasis added).

Intolerance is "an unwillingness to accept views, beliefs, or behavior that differ from one's own." But here's the deal—we should not accept beliefs that are not true. In refusing to do so, we are actually giving the world the tough love it needs so badly. What the world sees as bigotry is in reality our desire to see lost sinners saved from a very real hell.

||||||||||||

Let's approach the idea of exclusivity from a different angle. Pretend that I'm a parachute salesman. On display before you are four different types of parachutes. I fill you in about the benefits and drawbacks of each of the models.

Parachute One doesn't open.

Parachute Two opens, but under pressure the weak material always rips.

Parachute Three has faulty cords that under pressure always break.

Parachute Four never fails to open. It is totally reliable.

Which parachute will you choose? Well, that depends on whether or not you believe in gravity. If gravity is dismissed, which parachute is chosen won't matter to the prospective jumper. You can just choose the parachute that comes in your favorite color.

Unfortunately, gravity doesn't care whether you believe in it.

Late in September of 2020, I was deep in thought while walking down our stairs in the dark of the early morning. I wrongfully thought that I was on the bottom step, and I fell down the last step. It was just a one-step miscalculation, but with my five-foot, five-inch frame, the full distance of the fall was about six feet. It was a mere six feet, but it was a very fast and violent drop onto a hard wooden floor below. Fortunately, I didn't hit my head or break any bones. It just scared me and reminded me about the importance of holding on to the railing until I am safely at the bottom of the stairs.

Gravity refuses to compromise. It makes sure there are fearful consequences if we fall, even a short distance. Every year, hundreds of thousands of people die because of a miscalculation when it comes to gravity:

Falls are the second leading cause of unintentional injury deaths worldwide.

Each year an estimated 684,000 individuals die from falls globally of which over 80% are in low- and middle-income countries.

Adults older than 60 years of age suffer the greatest number of fatal falls.

37.3 million falls that are severe enough to require medical attention occur each year.[2]

Shrouded in darkness, the world forgets to hold on to the railing. Most people make a massive miscalculation when it comes to God's moral law. They hardly bring it into account when they have thoughts of God (see Rom. 7:7, 13). However, what sinners do with the Savior depends on their understanding of the effect of God's law—a law that's even stronger than the law of gravity.

Fortunately, the law is written on people's hearts (see Rom. 2:15). Sinners intuitively know it exists and that it is right in its demands. What they *don't* know are the dire consequences for violating its perfect precepts. Once they understand that, then having Jesus as Savior becomes a life-or-death, Heaven-or-hell issue.

And that brings us to my point. When it comes to the choice of parachutes, we need merely to use gravity as an educator. *Everything*, even a feather, falls toward the earth.

As one jumps out of the helicopter or airplane, the individual initially gains speed due to acceleration, which is caused by the earth's gravity. However, this speed does not keep on increasing indefinitely. There is a certain point at which the acceleration becomes zero; from that point onwards, the speed of the person is constant. The constant speed that a falling body achieves is called the terminal velocity. . . .

In a face-down position, the average value of terminal velocity is . . . 120 miles/hour.[3]

If we hit the ground at 120 mph, we are going to die. Gravity's refusal to compromise will make sure of that. Understanding that point should make us fearful, and that fear should cause us to be pointedly exclusive about our choice of parachutes. We must choose Parachute Four—the parachute that *never* fails.

Here now is our problem and the solution. The Bible says that no one truly understands God, sin, or the predicament in which they lie. We know that a law does exist, even if we choose to ignore it. But it is so easy to be blind to everything else, especially when it makes us look tolerant. The ungodly people in the world believe that all is well between them and their Creator—there is no wrath to come. They believe that there's nothing to fear, and that's why choosing the right religion isn't a matter of life and death to them. All that matters is love and tolerance—a willingness to accept other people's views, beliefs, or behaviors that differ from their own. Pick any parachute you want—but the world says you're a bigot and a bully if you say your parachute is better than anyone else's!

Look carefully at the following passage for the solution to our dilemma:

As it is written:

"There is none righteous, no, not one;
There is none who understands;
There is none who seeks after God.
They have all turned aside;
They have together become unprofitable;
There is none who does good, no, not one."
"Their throat is an open tomb;
With their tongues they have practiced deceit";
"The poison of asps is under their lips";
"Whose mouth is full of cursing and bitterness."
"Their feet are swift to shed blood;
Destruction and misery are in their ways;
And the way of peace they have not known."
"There is no fear of God before their eyes."

Now we know that whatever the law says, it says to those who are under the law, that every mouth may be stopped, and all the world may become guilty before God. (Rom. 3:10–19)

Scripture tells us about the universal sinful state of humanity. There is not one righteous person. We are all in big trouble because of our sin. God's wrath abides on us and divine justice is waiting to damn us (see Mark 16:16; John 3:36). We are in great and mortal danger. But again, no one understands. They think all is well. There's no fear of God before their eyes.

But the law of God shows sinners their danger. Like gravity, the law can function as an educator. That's why Paul calls it a "tutor" to bring us to Christ (see Gal. 3:24). And the way to show sinners their need of the Savior is to put them into an imaginary 120 mph free fall. Hang them over their drop into eternity for a moment, and let fear do its work. Their good sense will then push aside the horribly faulty parachutes of other religions and choose the only one that can save them. They must be exclusive. Nothing else will do *if they want to live.* Jesus is the only One who can forgive sin:

> So He got into a boat, crossed over, and came to His own city. Then behold, they brought to Him a paralytic lying on a bed. When Jesus saw their faith, He said to the paralytic, "Son, be of good cheer; your sins are forgiven you."
>
> And at once some of the scribes said within themselves, "This Man blasphemes!"
>
> But Jesus, knowing their thoughts, said, "Why do you think evil in your hearts? For which is easier, to say, 'Your sins are forgiven you,' or to say, 'Arise and walk'? But that you may know that the Son of Man has power on earth to forgive sins"—then He said to the paralytic, "Arise, take up your bed, and go to your house." And he arose and departed to his house.
>
> Now when the multitudes saw it, they marveled and glorified God, who had given such power to men. (Matt. 9:1–8)

The miraculous healing of the paralytic man was evidence that Jesus could forgive sin. And He can forgive sin because of the cross. Only His painful death could satisfy a wrath-filled law: "Nor is there salvation in any other, for there is no other name under heaven given among men by which we must be saved" (Acts 4:12).

What seems like intolerant bigotry toward other religions is the best news the world could ever hope to hear—that God did through the cross what they cannot do for themselves. He satisfied the law, cried out, "It is finished!" and then rose from the dead. Now He universally offers everlasting life as a free gift to all—Muslims, Hindus, Buddhists, atheists, agnostics, bigots, and even an intolerant world. And He—exclusively—is the only One who can make such an offer.

There are many who say they love God, and yet they reject Jesus. That's like saying they love the sun but reject the sunlight. Jesus is God come to the earth. He said, "For I have come down from heaven, not to do My own will, but the will of Him who sent Me" (John 6:38). To reject the Son is to reject the Father: "Who is a liar but he who denies that Jesus is the Christ? He is antichrist who denies the Father and the Son. Whoever denies the Son does not have the Father either; he who acknowledges the Son has the Father also" (1 John 2:22–23).

Witnessing Encounter

It is rare for Jehovah's Witnesses to openly admit that their religion is works based, that they are trying to earn their way into the kingdom of God. But they are. When I spoke with Mary and Sherry, I was delighted when Mary openly admitted that she believed works could get her to Heaven. Admission is the first step on the path to change.

RAY: Do you believe in an afterlife?
MARY: No.
RAY: This is it?

MARY: No, because I am one of the Jehovah's Witnesses, and we don't believe that.

RAY: The kingdom of God is coming to this earth, and God's will, will be done on this earth. Jehovah's will, will be done on this earth as it is in Heaven, the coming kingdom?

MARY: Yes, you are correct.

RAY: [addressing Sherry] Do you think there is an afterlife?

SHERRY: I think so. I do believe that there is a place where it's called Heaven, and I do believe that there is another place called hell.

RAY: Okay. There's a knife in my back, and I've got three minutes to live. I'm dying. How can I enter the kingdom? Tell me, please.

MARY: You can't enter the kingdom within three minutes. You have to abide by Bible principles until it comes.

RAY: You've got no hope for me? I have two and a half minutes now. What can I do? I'm dying. I'm scared to go to hell; please help me.

MARY: There's nothing I can do to help you with that one.

RAY: What about the thief on the cross? He was dying, but he got saved. He just turned to Jesus.

MARY: We don't believe in a cross. I don't. Where I believe, I don't believe in a cross.

RAY: Thief on the pole, he's dying. He turned to Jesus and he was saved—"Today you will be with Me in Paradise."[4] You know how he was saved?

MARY: No.

RAY: By the grace of God. He didn't *do* anything; he couldn't *go* anywhere. He was nailed to that pole, and he was saved by God's grace, and that's how you and I can be saved. It's not by works of righteousness that we do. How

can we *earn* everlasting life? It's a free gift of God—didn't
you know that?

MARY: We *earn* everlasting life by applying Bible principles,
and we keep doing what we gotta do. Then God will re-
ward us.

RAY: How much do you have to do to find everlasting life?

MARY: You don't gotta do much because all we do is knock
on people's doors and spread the word. That's our work;
that's my work. We both . . . we all have different beliefs,
but that's what I believe.

RAY: So how many doors do I have to knock on to earn everlasting life?

MARY: There's not a number because we're trying to save as
many people as possible.

RAY: So what say I knock on three doors. Will that get me to
the kingdom?

MARY: You've got to keep doing it; you can't just do it.
There's not a specific number.

RAY: A hundred doors?

MARY: There's not a specific number, there's not a specific
number, there's not a specific number.

RAY: Can you be sure of entering God's kingdom?

MARY: I'm sure because I have been learning stuff since I was
in diapers.

RAY: I'm going to share the gospel with our friend here
[Sherry], and you correct me afterward if you think I'm
wrong, okay? If I do anything wrong—you with me?

MARY: Got you.

RAY: Okay, now, do you think you're a good person?

SHERRY: I do. I do believe I'm a good person.

RAY: Jesus said there's none good but God, and do you know
how we can know if we're good? Just look at the Ten

Commandments. That's all we're going to do is look at those commandments that are written on your heart via your conscience. How many lies do you think you've told in your life?

SHERRY: I'm like, good at lying.

RAY: So what do you call someone who tells lies?

SHERRY: A liar.

RAY: Okay. Have you ever stolen something, even if it's small, in your whole life, irrespective of its value?

SHERRY: I did once. I stole like a candy when I was a child, but that's like the only thing.

RAY: You started early? You stole a candy when you were a child?

SHERRY: I wanted that candy.

RAY: Do you know that what you steal is irrelevant? If you open up my wallet and just take one dollar out, you're as much a thief as if you took ten dollars out. So what do you call someone who steals things?

SHERRY: A thief.

RAY: Have you ever used God's name in vain?

SHERRY: Um, yes, I have.

RAY: Would you use your mother's name as a cuss word?

SHERRY: Not in her face, but in my mind I have.

RAY: Whoa, that's breaking the fifth commandment, honor your father and mother. And when you use God's name as a cuss word it's called "blasphemy," punishable by death in the Old Testament. Once again, I appreciate your honesty and your humility. Jesus said if you look with lust, you commit adultery in the heart. Have you ever looked with lust?

SHERRY: No, I don't . . . I do lie.

MARY: Yeah, we all do.

SHERRY: We make mistakes. But I feel like we're human beings, and we learn [from] our mistakes; and so once we realize what we're doing and it's wrong, we, with some, do something about it and make sure not to do it again.

RAY: Okay, let me share what you can do about it, okay? I'm not judging you, but you've just told me you're a lying thief and a blasphemer, and I don't know if I can believe what you said about lust because you told me you're really good at lying. So if God judges you by the Ten Commandments on judgment day—we've looked at five—would you be innocent or guilty on judgment day of breaking those commandments?

SHERRY: Honestly, I would say I'm guilty. I can't say I'm innocent.

RAY: That's true. Heaven or hell?

SHERRY: Hell.

RAY: Now does that concern you?

SHERRY: It does. But if it comes to that point and I'm just accepting it, who knows if I do end up in hell or not.

RAY: Well, it horrifies me, and that's the last thing I want. I love you ladies; I care about you. The thought of you going to hell takes my breath away. It's so horrific. The Bible says God provided a way for us to be forgiven. Jesus suffered and died to take the punishment for our sins. You probably know that, but you may not know this. This is life changing. The Ten Commandments are called "the moral law"; you and I broke the law, Jesus paid the fine. That's why He said, "It is finished," just before He died. If you're in court and someone pays your fine, a judge can let you go even though you're guilty. He can say, "Ladies, there's a whole stack of speeding fines here. This is terribly serious, but someone's paid them, so you're free to go," and he can let you walk even though you're guilty. And he can do what is legal and right and just. Well, God can legally dismiss your case instantly because Jesus paid the fine in His life's blood. Even though we're guilty, God can let us live forever. He can take the death sentence off us and grant us everlasting life. Not because we're good but because God is good, and He's rich in mercy. And then Jesus rose from the dead and defeated death. Simply repent of your sins and say, "God, I'm sorry," and then turn from sin. Don't play the hypocrite and say I'm a Christian and lie and steal and fornicate; that's just deceiving yourself. You've got to be genuine in repentance. And then trust alone in Jesus. The moment you do that, God will give you everlasting life. At the moment, you're like I was for many years, like a man on the edge of a plane. He's ten thousand feet up and he's going to jump, and this is his plan: he's going to save himself by flapping his arms. I'd say to that person, don't do that, it's not going to work; trust the parachute. And so, don't look on your goodness to what's going to save you on the day of judgment. Don't try and save yourself; it's not going to work. Transfer your trust from yourself to the Savior. The minute you do that, you have God's promise that He will grant you everlasting life as a free gift—because you can't earn eternal life. The Bible says, "By grace you have been saved through faith, and that not of yourselves; it is the gift of God, not of works, lest anyone should boast."[5] It says that God saves us according to His mercy, not by our good works. Make sure you take heed to His words, "I am the way, the truth, and the life. No one comes to the Father except through Me."[6] Now tell me, Mary, where did I go wrong?

MARY: That's just your beliefs, you know.

RAY: Where did I go wrong?

MARY: You weren't wrong. I think everything you said was very knowledgeable.

RAY: Well, thank you for listening to me, ladies. Are you going to think about what we talked about?

MARY: Of course. I think about that, actually, every day.

RAY: And what about you, Sherry? You gonna think about it?

SHERRY: Yes, every day.

RAY: You ever get suicidal thoughts?

SHERRY: Umm, no.

RAY: You gave a little hesitation, so I'm going to give you a little booklet called *You're Not Alone: How to Battle Depression and Suicidal Thoughts*. Is that okay?

SHERRY: Yes. I mean, I would say I do go through depression, but it's never to the point where I want to be suicidal.

RAY: Well, let me just share something with you. If you lose your mom and dad or your grandma or grandpa, or even your dog, it can take you into deep depression, and a lot of people are taking their lives. So I'm going to give you this little booklet. Ladies, thanks for listening to me. I appreciate your patience with me.

I came away from that conversation shaking my head in disbelief. I had been able to witness to two Jehovah's Witnesses without contention. You can do this too. When you are a *Jesus* witness (as we all should be), you are giving testimony to His exclusivity. Never be afraid of being labeled "exclusive," because it's the truth—there is no other way except through Jesus. And we have to be brave enough to tell that to the world if we are going to be true and faithful.

5 | Jesus and the Crazy World

King Herod reigned as a king, but he was completely godless. He must have been insane. And so is this crazy world. King Herod and this world have similar approaches to Jesus. Let's take a look at Herod's life. But first, this is how Herod talked about Jesus:

> Now King Herod heard of [Jesus], for His name had become well known. And he said, "John the Baptist is risen from the dead, and therefore these powers are at work in him."
>
> Others said, "It is Elijah."
>
> And others said, "It is the Prophet, or like one of the prophets."
>
> But when Herod heard, he said, "This is John, whom I beheaded; he has been raised from the dead!" (Mark 6:14–16)

Herod had heard the rumors about a certain Jesus of Nazareth. Later on, Paul spoke about Him to another king and said, "This thing was not done in a corner" (Acts 26:26). Jesus had hit the Hebrew headlines, and John the Baptist had been the initial spark that spread Jesus's fame like fire. At the time, Herod was tetrarch of Galilee:

> Now in the fifteenth year of the reign of Tiberius Caesar, Pontius Pilate being governor of Judea, Herod being tetrarch of Galilee, his brother Philip tetrarch of Iturea and the region of Trachonitis, and Lysanias tetrarch of Abilene, while Annas and Caiaphas were high priests, the word of God came to John the son of Zacharias in the wilderness. And he went into all the region around the Jordan, preaching a baptism of repentance for the remission of sins, as it is written in the book of the words of Isaiah the prophet, saying:
>
> "The voice of one crying in the wilderness:
> 'Prepare the way of the Lord;
> Make His paths straight.
> Every valley shall be filled
> And every mountain and hill brought low;
> The crooked places shall be made straight
> And the rough ways smooth;
> And all flesh shall see the salvation of God.'" (Luke 3:1–6)

King Herod had royal blood in his veins. Like King David, he couldn't keep his hands off another man's wife. Also like David, he had married the woman in an effort to make adultery look morally legitimate. But it wasn't a legitimate marriage, and John the Baptist boldly told him so: "It is not lawful for you to have your brother's wife" (Mark 6:18). John reminded the king that he had violated God's law by taking Philip's wife. Herod then arrested John and put him in prison. Still, his illegitimate wife hated John and wanted to kill him, but Herod wouldn't let her (see v. 19) "because Herod feared John, knowing that he was a righteous and holy man, and he continually kept him safe. When he heard John [speak], he was very perplexed; but he enjoyed listening to him" (v. 20 AMP). Herod knew that John was holy, but Herod didn't like what the holy man said about the choices he made. Does that sound like anyone you know?

|||||||||||

Jesus aptly referred to Herod the king as "that fox" (Luke 13:32). Most of us think of the word *sly* when we hear that someone is like a fox, but it may have a deeper meaning:

> Jesus called Herod a fox after some Pharisees reported that Herod wanted to kill Jesus. Jesus' response challenged any such plans: "Tell Herod I've got work to do first." Jesus was not implying that Herod was sly, rather he was commenting on Herod's ineptitude, or inability, to carry out his threat. Jesus questioned the tetrarch's pedigree, moral stature and leadership, and put the tetrarch "in his place." This exactly fits the second rabbinic usage of "fox."
>
> When Jesus labeled Herod a fox, Jesus implied that Herod was not a lion. Herod considered himself a lion, but Jesus pointed out that Herod was the opposite of a lion. Jesus cut Herod down to size, and Jesus' audience may have had an inward smile of appreciation at a telling riposte.[1]

King Herod had inherited the sins of his not-so-nice father, Herod the Great. Instead of taking heed to the rebuke of John, he continued to give himself to sexual sin, just like his father had. Herod hardened his heart to John's wisdom. After he had John killed, he developed a similar fascination for Jesus that he'd had for John. After Jesus's arrest, Scripture says:

> As soon as [Pilate] knew that [Jesus] belonged to Herod's jurisdiction, he sent Him to Herod, who was also in Jerusalem at that time. Now when Herod saw Jesus, he was exceedingly glad; for he had desired for a long time to see Him, because he had heard many things about Him, and he hoped to see some miracle done by Him. Then he questioned Him with many words, but He answered him nothing. And the chief priests and scribes stood and vehemently

accused Him. Then Herod, with his men of war, treated Him with contempt and mocked Him, arrayed Him in a gorgeous robe, and sent Him back to Pilate. That very day Pilate and Herod became friends with each other, for previously they had been at enmity with each other. (Luke 23:7–12)

The godless world disagrees about so much, but one thing they can uniformly agree on is that they love the darkness and hate the light. For example, Herod and Pilate couldn't stand each other, but after they both mistreated Jesus, they became friends.

Here's the rest of this biblical soap opera. The lustful king was living in adultery with his brother's wife. She wanted to kill the preacher who pointed to their sin. Herod listened to John preach, but he continued to live in adultery. We are then privy to a royal party that turned into a bloody murder:

Then an opportune day came when Herod on his birthday gave a feast for his nobles, the high officers, and the chief men of Galilee. And when Herodias' daughter herself came in and danced, and pleased Herod and those who sat with him, the king said to the girl, "Ask me whatever you want, and I will give it to you." He also swore to her, "Whatever you ask me, I will give you, up to half my kingdom." (Mark 6:21–23)

Who was Herodias? She was Herod's lover. Both of them knew their marriage wasn't legitimate:

Herodias is the feminine form of Herod, which functions somewhat as a title for members of the Herodian dynasty. Historians indicate that Herod Antipas and Herodias had an affair of sorts while her husband Philip was visiting Rome. Herodias then agreed to leave her husband in order to become Herod Antipas's wife. Whether it was motivated by lust or was simply a power play, the new marriage was not honorable, and John the Baptist publicly denounced their adultery (Matthew 14:4).[2]

Herod is just like this insane world. His sin didn't keep him satisfied. He had already taken his brother's wife, but his eyes were full of adultery. He looked at his wife's seductive daughter, and lust exploded in his heart and stole what was left of his common sense. Sin tends to do that. Sin sent even a righteous man like King David into a frenzy, and it did so with Herod to a point of offering to give up half his kingdom.

Beware of lust. It blinds the soul. Lust won't take just half your kingdom; it wants your head on a plate. Don't let sin have its way. Ponder the path of your feet. Think about how God's eyes are in every place, beholding the evil and the good. Pray about what you think about and what you look at. Say with the psalmist, "Let the words of my mouth and the meditation of my heart be acceptable in Your sight, O LORD" (Ps. 19:14). Lust's pleasure will not only steal your common sense but also remove the fear of God from your heart. The two—lust and fear of God—cannot dwell together.

Herodias's daughter had been offered an open checkbook. She could have had untold riches, her own land, house, clothing—*anything* up to half his kingdom. For what would she ask? There's nothing like parental wisdom, so she asked her loving mother what she should do. And her wicked mother suggested a grisly murder:

> She went out and said to her mother, "What shall I ask?"
>
> And she said, "The head of John the Baptist!"
>
> Immediately she came in with haste to the king and asked, saying, "I want you to give me at once the head of John the Baptist on a platter."
>
> And the king was exceedingly sorry; yet, because of the oaths and because of those who sat with him, he did not want to refuse her. Immediately the king sent an executioner and commanded his head to be brought. And he went and beheaded him in prison, brought his head on a platter, and gave it to the girl; and the girl gave it to her mother. (Mark 6:24–28)

Notice what happened. Scripture uses the word *immediately* twice in this passage, also saying "she came in *with haste*" and said, "I want you to give me *at once*." How many horrific murders have been committed in the heat of the moment! Sin doesn't wait, as we see in the following modern-day story:

> A man who shot a woman dead and injured his own brother after they got his fast food order wrong has been handed a 130-year prison sentence.
>
> Andra Crockett killed 37-year-old Priscilla Aldridge and also shot his brother Kevin Thomas when they took the botched order back to his house in Blytheville, Arkansas.
>
> Crocket, aged 35, became extremely angry and argued with Aldridge when he was presented with the food. . . .
>
> According to one neighbor, Crockett looked at the food the duo had just brought back and said: "[Expletive], you know I don't like mayonnaise on my hamburger."[3]

We must strengthen ourselves in the fear of God. Satan seeks to sift us as wheat, and he surely had his way on that fateful day when a king gave his consent to the murder of the one Jesus pointed to as the greatest man ever born (see Matt. 11:11). When confronted with whether he should go back on his word, Herod chose instead to commit murder. He wanted to impress his guests. How insane . . . just like this insane world that gives Jesus a nod of approval by agreeing with the Golden Rule and celebrating His birth every year. But in the same breath people use His precious name as a cuss word. Like Herod, they love their sin and rush at hell as though it were Heaven. But the anger of Herodias was misdirected. John was merely the messenger. Her anger was really in response to God and His law, and He is the One she will face on judgment day.

Herod thought Jesus was John the Baptist resurrected from the dead, and the unsaved are similarly superstitious. They believe in space aliens, UFOs, Bigfoot, the Loch Ness monster, horoscopes, conspiracy theories, and other strange things. Satan doesn't care what the world believes, as long as it's not the truth. Just like King Herod, people would rather put their faith in anyone or anything but Jesus.

Witnessing Encounter

I was in Huntington Beach, California, in September of 2020, when I noticed a young man walking by. When I told him that we were filming a sequence for a TV program, he quickly agreed to step up to the microphone and talk about his thoughts on the afterlife.

RAY: Are you a well-read person? Are you educated?

SKYLAR: Yeah, I would say I'm fairly educated.

RAY: What's the world's most popular book of all time?

SKYLAR: Oh gosh, no idea.

RAY: The biggest selling book of all time.

SKYLAR: *The Great Gatsby*?

RAY: No.

SKYLAR: No?

RAY: Have another guess.

SKYLAR: Any Harry Potter books?

RAY: No, this leaves all those in the dust!

SKYLAR: Okay.

RAY: The Bible.

SKYLAR: The Bible?

RAY: Yes.

SKYLAR: Of course.

RAY: Have you ever read the Bible?

SKYLAR: Yeah, quite a bit I have.

RAY: Do you know its message?

SKYLAR: Uh, yeah.

RAY: Could you give me a synopsis of the whole Bible?

SKYLAR: It's basically just a backstory into the history of Christianity so you can become more familiar with, you know, what you're dealing with and what your beliefs are. In my opinion.

RAY: Well, let me give you my thought on the synopsis of the whole Bible. Old Testament: God promised to destroy death, our greatest enemy. New Testament tells us how He did it.

SKYLAR: Yeah.

RAY: Are you familiar with the apostle Paul?

SKYLAR: The impossible Paul?

RAY: The apostle Paul.

SKYLAR: No.

RAY: He wrote most of the New Testament. And it says the apostle Paul persuaded men "concerning Jesus from both the Law of Moses and the Prophets."[4] Are you familiar with the law of Moses?

SKYLAR: Yes.

RAY: That's the Ten Commandments.

SKYLAR: Yes.

RAY: Are you familiar with the prophets?

SKYLAR: No, not entirely.

RAY: Have you ever studied Bible prophecy?

SKYLAR: No, I have not.

RAY: So, I'm going to talk about Bible prophecy for a few moments because I want to convince you of something very important. This is what I want to convince you: I want to convince you you're in great danger, but you don't realize it. That's why you need Jesus. You need a Savior. You need someone who can wash away your sins. Let me tell you something. I'm going to sound a little weird at first. I love sports. I watch a lot of sports with my wife, but what we do with our favorite team, that's a rugby team, we go ahead and see who won the game and we don't watch it unless we win.

SKYLAR: Oh wow.

RAY: That's crazy, it seems, except for this reason: we don't like stress at our age—it's not good for you. It's good to know that our team won. So when the other team high-fives and gets a score, we just look at each other and smile because we know the future.

SKYLAR: Okay.

RAY: Now the Bible tells us the future. Do you think any human being knows the future?

SKYLAR: No.

RAY: No, we don't, do we? Weather forecasters think they know what's going to happen tomorrow, but often a parade is rained on because they get it wrong. We don't know what's going to happen in five minutes. This is California; the ground could open up and we could be swallowed by an earthquake! So let me share a few Bible prophecies with you.

SKYLAR: Sure.

RAY: Do you think we're living in fearful times?

SKYLAR: Yes.

RAY: The Bible says the last days shall be perilous times.[5]

SKYLAR: Yes.

RAY: Men's hearts would fail them for fear of that which is coming upon the earth. We're seeing things like pestilence or plagues on the earth just like the Bible says.

SKYLAR: Yes.

RAY: These are apocalyptic times. The CDC said that in June of 2020, nearly 11 percent of Americans seriously considered committing suicide. That's how scary it is for a lot of people.

SKYLAR: Yes, it's terrifying.

RAY: But when you're a Christian you know the future because the Bible gives us undeniable prophecies. Let me give you a few of them. In Matthew 24 and Luke 21, Jesus told us what was going to happen to the Jewish nation. Jesus predicted the destruction of Jerusalem, and years later in AD 70 the city was besieged and the Jews were scattered throughout the earth. For the next 2,000 years the Jews didn't have a homeland, yet they retained their identity as a people until 1948 when they became their own nation. *Live Science* said, "In the millennia afterwards the Jewish dispersion spread throughout the world. It wasn't until the establishment of the modern state of Israel in 1948 that the Jewish people had a homeland again."[6] In Luke 21, verse 24, two thousand years earlier, Jesus had prophesied, "And they will fall by the edge of the sword, and be led away captive into all nations." Then in 1967 the Jews actually possessed Jerusalem. Again, in verse 24 Jesus had foretold, "And Jerusalem will be trampled by Gentiles until the times of the Gentiles are fulfilled." But right up until 1967, Jerusalem was under gentile control. So the Bible prophecy that Jesus spoke has been fulfilled. You know who gentiles are?

SKYLAR: No.

RAY: That's non-Jewish people.

SKYLAR: Okay.

RAY: And Jerusalem was in the hands of non-Jews right up until 1967 when the Jews got Jerusalem back for the first time in 2,000 years, bringing into culmination that we're in the end of this age, just before the coming of Christ. And the Bible gives a whole stack of other signs; it says there would be lawlessness and rebellious youth.

SKYLAR: Yes.

RAY: Those signs have always been around, but Jerusalem is the sign to look for. So that seals the Bible as the Word of God and shows us the fingerprint of God all over the Bible. We've looked at the prophets to substantiate that the Bible's the Word of God, and now we're going to look at the law of Moses. You said you are a good person?

SKYLAR: Yes.

RAY: I'm going to try and change your mind about that.

SKYLAR: Okay.

RAY: You know how I'm going to do it?

SKYLAR: How so?

RAY: I'm going to give you a moral speedometer. Ever driven the highway and you've seen those big speedometers saying that you're going 56 . . . you're going 57. Why do you think they do that?

SKYLAR: So that you know to slow down.

RAY: Yes, they want you to slow down. It gives you a gauge to go by to see how much you're infringing the law. Do you ever take notice of those things?

SKYLAR: Yes.

RAY: You do?

SKYLAR: Oh yes.

RAY: Of course, a lot of people don't.

SKYLAR: I'm not getting a ticket.

RAY: Yes, a lot of people don't. So I ask them this: "If there's an officer on a motorbike sitting at the base of that speedometer, does that change things?" They say, "Oh yeah," because they know the law is going to be enforced; it's not just a sign. There's a human being that stands for right and wrong, and he's going to grab you and you're going to be prosecuted. So I'm going to share the moral speedometer with you, the Ten Commandments, to show you that you're in transgression of God's law and you're in big trouble. Are you ready?

SKYLAR: Sure.

RAY: Can you be honest with me?

SKYLAR: Sure.

RAY: Here we go. . . . How many lies have you told in your life?

SKYLAR: Probably tens of thousands.

RAY: Okay, what do you call someone who's told tens of thousands of lies?

SKYLAR: An impulsive liar.

RAY: Yes, so what are you?

SKYLAR: An impulsive liar.

RAY: You're still a good person?

SKYLAR: Yes, supposedly so.

RAY: Have you ever stolen something even if it's small?

SKYLAR: Yes.

RAY: So what do you call someone who steals things?

SKYLAR: A thief.

RAY: So what are you?

SKYLAR: A thief, I suppose.

RAY: No, you're not; you're a lying thief, Skylar.

SKYLAR: [laughs]

RAY: Now do you still think you're a good person?

SKYLAR: Oh, now you're making me think a little bit.

RAY: That's what the law does; it gives us light. Have you ever used God's name in vain?

SKYLAR: A few times I have.

RAY: Now why would you do that? I can understand why you'd use a filthy word if you slam your finger in a door. You want to express disgust, so you use a filthy word.

SKYLAR: Of course.

RAY: Why would you take the holy name of God and use it in place of that filthy word?

SKYLAR: Out of anger, I guess.

RAY: Out of anger?

SKYLAR: Yes.

RAY: But why don't you stay with a filthy word? Why do you take *God's* name? Any idea?

SKYLAR: Who knows?

RAY: Why would you take the name of Jesus Christ and use it the same way?

SKYLAR: Yes, true.

RAY: You know who knows?

SKYLAR: Who?

RAY: God knows, and He tells us why. But before we look at why we do it, let me ask another question, and think before you answer. Would you ever use your mother's name as a cuss word?

SKYLAR: No.

RAY: Tell me why not.

SKYLAR: Disrespect.

RAY: Disrespect.

SKYLAR: Yes.

RAY: Because you love your mother, you respect her.

SKYLAR: Yes.

RAY: But you don't love the God who gave you life and your mother. You've taken His holy name and disrespected it; used it as a cuss word to express disgust, and that's called "blasphemy." It's so serious, it's punishable by death. Now let me tell you why we do it. Jesus told us in John chapter 7 that the world hates Him (and there's no greater evidence that we hate God than that we use His name as a cuss word). He said, "The world . . . hates Me because I testify of it that its works are evil."[7] It's the same reason criminals hate the police; they'll kill a police officer not because of who he is but because of what he stands for: that which is right and good and just.

SKYLAR: Yes.

RAY: Still think you're a good person?

SKYLAR: Kind of a good person now, I suppose.

RAY: Slowing down, isn't it? You're getting a contrast.

SKYLAR: Yes.

RAY: I appreciate your honesty. Jesus said, "Whoever looks at a woman to lust for her has already committed adultery with her in his heart."[8] Have you ever looked at a woman with lust?

SKYLAR: Oh yes, out here a few times.

RAY: Have you had sex before marriage?

SKYLAR: Yes.

RAY: That's called "fornication." So here's a summation. Skylar, I'm not judging you. I'm letting you judge yourself, okay? *You* look at the speedometer and see how you're doing. You've told me you're a lying, thieving, blasphemous, fornicating adulterer at heart.

SKYLAR: [nervous laughter]

RAY: And you're also self-righteous in saying you're a good person when you're not. So here's the big question (this is where we're going with this): If God judges you by the

Ten Commandments—we've looked at four of them—on judgment day, are you going to be innocent or guilty?

SKYLAR: Gosh. Apparently guilty.

RAY: Heaven or hell?

SKYLAR: Hopefully Heaven . . . maybe hell.

RAY: Well, the Bible says definitely hell. It says that all liars will have their part in the lake of fire. No thief, no blasphemer, no adulterer will inherit the kingdom of God. Skylar, do you know what death is, according to the Bible?

SKYLAR: End of life? I don't understand exactly.

RAY: It's called *wages*. Have you ever heard the famous Bible verse, "The wages of sin is death"?

SKYLAR: No.

RAY: It's in Romans 6:23, "The wages of sin is death." God is so serious about sin that He's paying you the wages of death for your sins. It's like when a judge in a court of law looks at a heinous criminal who's murdered three girls and slit their throats, and he says, "You've *earned* the death sentence. This is what you deserve. This is your wages." And God says sin is so serious He's put you on death row to be executed. You're going to receive capital punishment because your sin is so serious in the eyes of a holy God. What I'm trying to do is show you that seriousness, to show you're in terrible danger. Can you see that?

SKYLAR: Yes, I actually do now.

RAY: If death seized upon you today, you'd be damned, and I'd hate that to happen. Death is an arresting officer that's going to drag you before the judge of the universe, to stand trial for violation of His law, and hell is God's prison and there's no parole. So I am horrified at the thought of you, Skylar, a human being that loves life, ending up damned by almighty God. Remember what I said earlier? I quoted what the apostle Paul did. He persuaded men concerning Jesus both out of the law of Moses (the Ten Commandments) and out of the prophets. We look to the prophets to substantiate the truth of Scripture, and we're looking at the law of Moses to show you need a Savior; you need Jesus. Now most people know that Jesus died on the cross for the sin of the world, but they don't know this: the Ten Commandments are called the moral law. You and I broke the law; Jesus came and paid the fine. That's what happened on the cross.

SKYLAR: Okay.

RAY: Skylar, if you're in court and someone pays your fine, a judge can let you go, even though you're guilty. He can say, "Skylar, there's a stack of speeding fines here, this is deadly serious, but someone's paid them; you're free to go!" Even though you're guilty, he can let you go because someone paid your fine, and he can do that which is legal and right and just. Can you see that?

SKYLAR: Yes.

RAY: And God can *legally* let you live forever, take the death sentence off you, because Jesus paid the fine in full. He can do that which is legal and right and just. Jesus paid the fine on the cross, therefore you can walk freely, not receiving God's just condemnation for your sins. Is this making sense?

SKYLAR: Yes.

RAY: Skylar, then Jesus rose from the dead. The Bible says it was not possible that death could hold Him, and now the Bible tells us that God offers everlasting life to the whole of humanity—whosoever will may come. Whoever calls upon the name of the Lord shall be saved. The Bible says, "For God so loved the world that He gave His only begotten Son, that whoever believes in Him should not perish but have everlasting life."⁹ And the way to receive everlasting life is through two things, according to the Bible: you must repent of your sins. Do you know what repentance is?

SKYLAR: Repentance?

RAY: Yes.

SKYLAR: Yes, you have to repent. You have to ask for forgiveness.

RAY: Well, it's more than asking for forgiveness; it's actually turning from sin. You can't say, "I'm a Christian," but you fornicate, lie, steal, lust, and blaspheme. That's playing the hypocrite, just deceiving yourself. So you must be genuine. And the second thing you must do is this: you must put your trust in Jesus Christ for your eternal salvation. At the moment, you're like a man on the edge of a plane, 10,000 feet up. He's not wearing a parachute, and this is his plan: when he jumps, he's going to flap his arms and try to save himself. But I'd say to that man, "Don't do that! Trust the parachute!" It's so simple—trust the parachute. So don't trust in your goodness to save yourself on judgment day. It's not going to work. You've got a multitude of sins like the rest of us. Simply transfer your trust from yourself to the Savior, and the second you do that, you've got a promise from the God who cannot lie that He'll remit your sins. The Bible says it's impossible for God to lie. That means you can trust everything He says. He'll grant everlasting life as a free gift, open the eyes of your understanding, and give you a new heart with new desires, so that you love righteousness instead of sin. At the moment, you drink iniquity like water; you love fornication, love pornography, you love that which is wrong. But God says that He will so transform your heart, you'll love that which is right, which is a miracle for sin-loving sinners. Skylar, are you going to think about what we talked about today?

SKYLAR: Of course, I'll probably think about it for the next few hours, and then think about it a week from now, and then think about it a month from now.

RAY: Well, I don't want you to just think about it; I want you to *do* something about your eternal salvation.

SKYLAR: Yes.

RAY: And you can leave here and die, have a heart attack, aneurism in your sleep.

SKYLAR: Hopefully not.

RAY: You could get a pestilence or a plague. You just don't know what's going to happen. Every day 350,000 people die, so I'd like to put the fear of God into your heart and show you this is deadly serious. The fear of God is the beginning of wisdom, and you'll not let go of your beloved sins until you see you're in great danger. So you have to do two things to be saved: you must repent, and you must trust alone in Jesus. When are you going to do that?

SKYLAR: I'll start today.

RAY: You serious?

SKYLAR: Yes.

RAY: May I pray with you?

SKYLAR: Sure.

RAY: Father, I pray for Skylar, that this day he'll see sin in its true light and he'll understand the cross—that Christ died for us while we're still sinners. While we're yet sinners. Such is your love for us. I pray you'll grant him genuine repentance, that he'll turn from sin and willfully place his faith in Jesus and pass from death to life because of your great mercy. In Jesus's name we pray, amen. Skylar, stay there. I'm going to bring you a little booklet called *Save Yourself Some Pain*. It's got principles of Christian growth in it. Thank you so much for listening to me. It's meant a lot to me that you listened.

According to his own summation, the young man I spoke with was in sore need of God's wonderful mercy. What a joy it was to see him looking at the book I had just given him as he walked away.

6 | Jesus and Authority

Despite the poor quality of the picture from the surveillance camera, it was easy to see the figure of a youth hold up a gun, aim it at close range toward a police squad car, shoot multiple times, and run.

It was Saturday, September 12, 2020. Inside the car were two Los Angeles County Sheriff's Department deputies from the city of Compton. One was a thirty-one-year-old mother of a six-year-old boy. One bullet ripped through her jaw, but despite horrific injuries she got on the radio and called for help, provided medical care to the other wounded officer, and then moved him to a place of safety. The twenty-four-year-old had been struck in the forehead, arm, and hand. A graphic photo of the immediate aftermath of the attack showed the female officer covered in blood while giving medical help to her injured partner.[1]

The police officers were shot because of the *authority* they held as officers of the law. If they had no authority to arrest and prosecute criminals, they wouldn't have been in danger.

Other professionals have a different type of authority that rarely provokes hatred. We seek out certain specialists not because they *have* authority but because they *are* an authority on a particular subject. We look to a chiropractor for help with a bad back, a dentist to take care of our teeth, and a mechanic to work on our car. In the same way, we must go to Jesus for the issues of life and death. He is the authority on life because He is its author. As Peter once said to a crowd of people, "But you killed the Prince (Author, Originator, Source) of life, whom God raised [bodily] from the dead. To this [fact] we are witnesses [for we have seen the risen Christ]" (Acts 3:15 AMP).

Jesus Himself claimed His authority boldly: "And Jesus came and spoke to them, saying, 'All authority has been given to Me in heaven and on earth'" (Matt. 28:18).

Humble sinners who see their need for God's forgiveness will seek Jesus because He is the only one who has the power on earth to forgive sins. They don't feel threatened by His authority. However, the proud are contemptuous toward Him because He is a threat to their pleasures. They despise His name and gladly substitute it for a filthy word. He condemns lust, adultery, fornication, lying, theft, blasphemy, anger, hatred, greed, and even every idle word they speak, and they hate Him for it: "The world cannot hate you, but it hates Me because I testify of it that its works are evil" (John 7:7).

Drivers often ignore large speedometer signs on the roadside telling them they are breaking the law. But the warning is rarely ignored if an *officer* is sitting on his motorbike beside the speedometer. Drivers slow down because the law now has authority. They fear that it will be enforced.

Our message for this lawless world is that God stands by His Word, and we know from Scripture that He will enforce it: "When the Son of Man comes in His glory, and all the holy angels with Him, then He will sit on the throne of His glory. All the nations will be gathered before Him, and He will separate them one from another, as a shepherd divides his sheep from the goats" (Matt. 25:31–32).

When we talk with a specialist, we want him to speak with confidence. We don't want a surgeon to say, "I'm really not too sure about how I will operate." The last thing I'd want to hear my surgeon say is "I *hope* I can help." Yikes! We want to hear our specialists say, "I *know* what the problem is, and I will fix it for you." Such talk breeds trust—and *trust* is what's needed. It's not wise to have surgery by a surgeon we don't trust.

When the humble heard Jesus speak with a confident authority, it bred trust. They *believed* on Him. And He spoke with such confidence, He both thrilled and confounded His hearers:

> Then He went down to Capernaum, a city of Galilee, and was teaching them on the Sabbaths. And they were astonished at His teaching, for His word was with authority. Now in the synagogue there was a man who had a spirit of an unclean demon. And he cried out with a loud voice, saying, "Let us alone! What have we to do with You, Jesus of Nazareth? Did You come to destroy us? I know who You are—the Holy One of God!"
>
> But Jesus rebuked him, saying, "Be quiet, and come out of him!" And when the demon had thrown him in their midst, it came out of him and did not hurt him. Then they were all amazed and spoke among themselves, saying, "What a word this is! For with authority and power He commands the unclean spirits, and they come out." And the report about Him went out into every place in the surrounding region. (Luke 4:31–37)

Demons bowed to Jesus's authority. He spoke to the weather, and it obeyed Him. Disease left when He told it to, and to Him alone the grim reaper bowed the knee. At the conclusion of the Sermon on the Mount, Scripture says, "And so it was, when Jesus had ended these sayings, that the people were astonished at His teaching, for He taught them as one having authority, and not as the scribes" (Matt. 7:28–29). Jesus never denied His authority.

Back-to-Back Advice

It is a great relief to find an expert who can put his finger on the cause of some ailment. For some reason (probably genetic), I have had a weakness in my lower spine since I was a teenager. It's a very common condition called spondylolisthesis.

One day I started getting sharp pains in my left foot. When I asked a chiropractor why he thought it was happening, he answered with an air of authority. He said, "It's your back that's causing it. I'm sure of that." I was mystified. It was my foot, not my back that was giving me pain. But he explained that feet and backs are connected by a complex nervous system and that all I needed to do to fix the problem was to regularly sit with my knees leaning toward the left side of my body. I made a habit of doing that during my regular prayer time, and it fixed the problem. Almost daily when I pray, I think of my chiropractor friend with gratitude for his expertise.

And more than daily—minute by minute—I am so grateful that Jesus had authority over death: "I am he that liveth, and was dead; and, behold, I am alive for evermore, Amen; and have the keys of hell and of death" (Rev. 1:18 KJV).

Look at how a Roman centurion revealed his faith as he understood the authority Jesus possessed:

> Now when Jesus had entered Capernaum, a centurion came to Him, pleading with Him, saying, "Lord, my servant is lying at home paralyzed, dreadfully tormented."
>
> And Jesus said to him, "I will come and heal him."
>
> The centurion answered and said, "Lord, I am not worthy that You should come under my roof. But only speak a word, and my servant will be healed. For I also am a man under authority, having soldiers under me. And I say to this one, 'Go,' and he goes; and to another, 'Come,' and he comes; and to my servant, 'Do this,' and he does it."
>
> When Jesus heard it, He marveled, and said to those who followed, "Assuredly, I say to you, I have not found such great faith, not even in Israel!" (Matt. 8:5–10)

Our God-Given Authority

Samuel Chadwick (1860–1932) once said, "The Church is the Body of Christ, and the Spirit is the Spirit of Christ. He fills the Body, directs its movements, controls its members, inspires its wisdom, supplies its strength. He guides into truth, sanctifies its agents, and empowers for witnessing. The Spirit has never abdicated His authority nor relegated His power."[2]

We are Christ's body on earth, and when we speak about the character and promises of God, an unbelieving world is more likely to believe what we're telling them if we speak with authority. This must be thoroughly mixed with an evident humility. The fountain of our faith is love for sinners, and God forbid that we would ever speak with an authority that is mixed with a pharisaic condescension: "A servant of the Lord must not quarrel but be gentle to all, able to teach, patient, in humility correcting those who are in opposition, if God perhaps will grant them repentance, so that they may know the truth" (2 Tim. 2:24–25).

Look at the humility of Peter after he and John were used by God to heal a lame man:

> Now as the lame man who was healed held on to Peter and John, all the people ran together to them in the porch which is called Solomon's, greatly amazed. So when Peter saw it, he responded to the people: "Men of Israel, why do you marvel at this? Or why look so intently at us, as though by our own power or godliness we had made this man walk? The God of Abraham, Isaac, and Jacob, the God of our fathers, glorified His Servant Jesus, whom you delivered up and denied in the presence of Pilate, when he was determined to let Him go. But you denied the Holy One and the Just, and asked for a murderer to be granted to you, and killed the Prince of life, whom God raised from the dead, of which we are witnesses." (Acts 3:11–15)

After the giving of the Holy Spirit, the disciples became specialists. They were sought out because they had the power to heal the sick. But it wasn't the first time the disciples had exercised supernatural authority. Before His death and resurrection, Jesus sent out seventy disciples to heal and drive out demons. Look at what Jesus said to them after they returned from laboring in the harvest fields:

> Then the seventy returned with joy, saying, "Lord, even the demons are subject to us in Your name."
> And He said to them, "I saw Satan fall like lightning from heaven. Behold, I give you the authority to trample on serpents and scorpions, and over all the power of the enemy, and nothing shall by any means hurt you. Nevertheless do not rejoice in this, that the spirits are subject to you, but rather rejoice because your names are written in heaven." (Luke 10:17–20)

Jesus told them that He was present when Satan exalted himself and fell from Heaven through pride:

> How you are fallen from heaven,
> O Lucifer, son of the morning!
> How you are cut down to the ground,
> You who weakened the nations! (Isa. 14:12)

Many lesser authorities fall because of pride. We should all take note of this. Our safeguard against it is to realize that we can do nothing on our own. Peter had rightly asked those who exalted him, "Why look so intently at us, as though by our own power or godliness we had made this man walk?" By knowing that God was the one working, Peter guarded himself from pride.

Pride is like a stubborn weed that grows without water through a crack in hardened concrete. No matter how hard we try to stop sinful thoughts, they find a way into our sinful hearts. We kiss our own hands, whisper compliments to ourselves, and pat ourselves on the back for little or no reason. The trumpet is close to our lips the moment we put money in the plate—because there's a proud Pharisee in every one of us. Like a stubborn bulldog on a leash, pride will take the lead if we let it. The lust of the flesh, the lust of the eyes, and the pride of life are a threefold cord that's not easily broken. If someone hands me the rose of a compliment, I have to handle it carefully lest I injure myself on the thorns of pride. My sinful flesh is easily penetrated.

Bible commentator Matthew Henry explains the humility that must accompany any God-given authority:

> Observe the difference in the manner of working the miracles. Our Lord always spoke as having Almighty power, never hesitated to receive the greatest honor that was given to him on account of his Divine miracles. But the apostles referred all to the Lord, and refused to receive any honor, except as his undeserving instruments. This shows that Jesus was one with the Father, and co-equal with Him; while the apostles knew that they were weak, sinful men, and dependent for every thing on Jesus, whose power effected the cure. Useful men must be very humble. Not unto us, O Lord, not unto us, but to thy name, give glory. Every crown must be cast at the feet of Christ. The apostle showed the Jews the greatness of their crime, but would not anger or drive them to despair. Assuredly, those who reject, refuse, or deny Christ, do it through ignorance; but this can in no case be an excuse.[3]

It is in that humble spirit that we speak about the terrible wrath of God, His perfect holiness, His love and faithfulness, and sinners' moral condition and their fate if they die in their sins. They will *certainly* be damned. But we can assure the lost with absolute certainty that if they repent and call on the name of Jesus, they will find peace with God. We say these things based on the authority of the Word of God. There's no higher authority.

Someone once wrote to me to ask a cynical question. I'd like to say this has happened only once, but I've received all kinds of questions that mock the authority of God.

I have a question for you. If you were born on a remote island, where you only had your instinct to tell you how to survive. Assuming your parents were the same, and they have no recollection of how they got there, and none of you can speak and have never seen human beings before other than yourselves. How on this big blue earth would you ever believe in Jesus? And in that case, you would probably be doomed to eternal fire as well. Well, the funny thing is . . . this is a real situation that DOES occur. And there are tribes all around the world even today that are completely clueless of Jesus or any other religious figure in this world. How could you explain the sheer stupidity of thinking that they deserve to go to hell, even though they have never had a chance to believe in the first place? Good luck.

We don't need luck to answer the questions the world asks because we have the Word of God. That's our expert authority. It tells us that every sane person on this earth has a God-given, society-shaped conscience. When we commit adultery, rape, or murder, when we lie, steal, blaspheme, or do anything sinful, we do it *knowing* right from wrong. That means that God is justified in condemning us. This is exemplified in criminal law. According to the Cornell Law School website:

> *Mens Rea* refers to criminal intent. The literal translation from Latin is "guilty mind." . . . A *mens rea* refers to the state of mind statutorily required in order to convict a particular defendant of a particular crime. See, e.g. Staples v. United States, 511 US 600 (1994). Establishing the *mens rea* of an offender is usually necessary to prove guilt in a criminal trial. The prosecution typically must prove beyond reasonable doubt that the defendant committed the offense with a culpable state of mind.[4]

It's because we care about those who are in danger of damnation that we send missionaries (often in peril of their lives) to share the good news of the gospel—that God can forgive them and freely grant them everlasting life through repentance and faith in Jesus. Only He has authority on earth to forgive sin.

Witnessing Encounter

I spoke with a young man named Mario around July 2020. But first, I want to share a testimony from someone named Nick who left a comment under Mario's video:

> I've been an atheist most of my life. I then became a Satanist and signed my name in blood on a hand written contract (I wrote it) then burned the paper. The past five days I've begun looking further into Christianity and our Lord, Jesus Christ. Three days ago I registered to be Baptized in the name of Jesus Christ on Jan 2nd and the past hour this evening multiple different testimonies and this video have all brought me to tears which I didn't fully understand until the end of this video when [Mario] explained why. I immediately started crying again. I've been alone struggling in many ways and have committed every sin short of murder. For years I've been trying to fight suicidal ideations and asking my family for help. Everyone says they'll help but then nothing. When I was crying I heard a subtle voice say, "I love you. I'm with you." I'm so grateful to have finally found the one who cares most about me and all of us. I'm so sorry for all the times I spoke negatively of God. I don't think it's a coincidence this has happened on Christmas day. God bless you all. I love each and every one of you.

And now my conversation with Mario.

RAY: So, Mario, are you spiritual?

MARIO: Yes.

RAY: What do you mean by that?

MARIO: The way I grew up, my heart was in my neighborhood . . . but my love—I've always been loyal to love. I've always known that. But it deceived me. I confused the two. If you confuse the two, it lets you down. You have to pick yourself up.

RAY: Is that what you mean by spiritual? Self-improvement?

MARIO: Yes.

RAY: Or talking about God?

MARIO: Self-improvement, that's what I believe in. I believe all religions have a universal meaning. I believe in the power of the universe. I believe that we are all just humans and we are all here to spread love, and that's all I got to do.

RAY: So do you think God created everything? Do you think evolution created everything?

MARIO: We can never know, ever.

RAY: Oh, you may not be able to know, but I know.

MARIO: You can know within.

RAY: You hear that, Mario? I know. You don't know.

MARIO: Yes.

RAY: You can't say we can never know; that's limiting your knowledge. Do you ever think about how amazing life is?

MARIO: I do.

RAY: I mean, look at the blueness of the sky, and the sun. You ever think about the sun and how incredible it is? It's 93 million miles away and it's just warm enough to ripen your tomatoes. Any closer, we're all dead. Farther away, we're all dead. You ever think about how amazing that is?

MARIO: I do.

RAY: How did it get there?

MARIO: I had to learn it myself. I had to go within, and nobody can teach it for you. You have to go within, and you can unlock the secrets to the universe if your loyalty lies in the love for yourself. That's it.

RAY: You love yourself?

MARIO: I do.

RAY: You love God?

MARIO: I love God. But in my mind, God is the entire universe.

RAY: Well, that's called pantheism. There's a difference between a painter and a painting. You don't love the painting; you love the painter because he's the genius that created the painting. So if you love creation, you're setting your affection on the creation rather than the Creator, and that's called "inordinate affection." It's the wrong order of affections. If your mom gave you a gift and you loved the gift more than you love your mom, there's something wrong. You should be saying, "Hey, Mom, thanks for this car. I'm grateful to you, not to the car. I'm grateful to you for the gift." Make sense?

MARIO: I personally know who I am and why I'm here. I found my purpose from within. I know that to be true. I've never lost that my entire life. I've been the same person. You need love. You can't be a man without love. You have to separate yourself from love in order to find that for yourself. Nobody else can do it for you, that's the point.

RAY: You trust yourself?

MARIO: I do.

RAY: Let me ask you a question, spell the word *shop*.

MARIO: S-H-O-P.

RAY: What do you do when you come to a green light?

MARIO: G-O.

RAY: Good work. Spell the word *silk*.

MARIO: S-I-L-K.

RAY: What do cows drink?

MARIO: M-I-L-K.

RAY: No, they drink water. Never trust yourself because we are easily deceived. The Bible says, "He who trusts in his own heart is a fool."[5] A lot of people are dead because

they trusted their own heart; they made judgments—
"I can beat that truck and overtake this car," but they
couldn't—wrong judgment. Let me ask you another question. You said your concept of God, He is the universe?

MARIO: Yes.

RAY: Do you think God is happy with you or angry at you?

MARIO: Depending on what you do, God will love you for it
either way. That's what I believe in.

RAY: So how are you doing morally?

MARIO: As long as you stay true to yourself, God will love
you. It doesn't matter what you do as long as you know in
your heart you're doing it for the right reason—love. You
have nothing to worry about in this world whatsoever; it's
called faith.

RAY: Let's see how you're doing. Do you think you're a good
person?

MARIO: Yes.

RAY: How many lies have you told in your life?

MARIO: I've lost count.

RAY: What do you call someone who's told lies?

MARIO: A liar.

RAY: So you've blown that one. Have you ever stolen something, even if it's small?

MARIO: Yes.

RAY: What do you call someone who steals?

MARIO: A liar.

RAY: A thief.

MARIO: If you deny that you lie, steal, cheat, and deceive,
you become those things, and that's what you have to
understand as human. Is that you can't lose yourself in
yourself because that's the double-edged sword of love.

It's out there, you just got to find it for yourself in order to truly know what it is, and I just want to push that to everybody.

RAY: Mario, you were saying that you found yourself. What are mankind's origins, where do we come from?

MARIO: Women.

RAY: Yes, but I mean originally. I don't mean from your mother. What's the origin of humanity?

MARIO: Authenticity and love.

RAY: No, the origin, where do we come from? What was in the beginning?

MARIO: Man and woman.

RAY: Yes, but before man and woman, who created man and woman?

MARIO: A higher power.

RAY: Who was that?

MARIO: God.

RAY: Why do we exist as human beings?

MARIO: To love.

RAY: Where are you going when you die?

MARIO: Whatever you did here, it depends.

RAY: That's true. Now, third commandment, "You shall not take God's name in vain." Have you ever used God's name in vain?

MARIO: [nods]

RAY: Would you use your mother's name as a cuss word?

MARIO: Never.

RAY: Never, because you honor her. But you haven't loved and honored God. You've used His name as a filthy word to express disgust, which is called "blasphemy." It's so serious, it's punishable by death in the Old Testament. I appreciate your honesty and your patience with me. Jesus said that if you look at a woman and lust for her, you commit adultery with her in your heart. Have you ever looked at a woman with lust?

MARIO: Yes, I'm a man.

RAY: Ever have sex before marriage?

MARIO: Yes, I'm a man.

RAY: So, Mario, I'm not judging you, you judge yourself. But you've told me you're a lying, thieving, blasphemous, fornicating adulterer at heart, and you have to face God on judgment day. If He judges you by the Ten Commandments—we've looked at four—are you going to be innocent or guilty?

MARIO: Guilty.

RAY: Heaven or hell?

MARIO: Hell.

RAY: Now does that concern you?

MARIO: Deep down, yes.

RAY: It horrifies me. We've just met. I love you; I care about you. The thought of you going to hell just breaks my heart. Do you know what death actually is? According to the Bible?

MARIO: Ultimate enlightenment.

RAY: Well, no, it's "wages." It says, "The wages of sin is death."[6] God's given you death as wages for your sin. He's paying you in death. He's giving you capital punishment, like a judge who looks at a heinous criminal who's raped three girls and then murdered them and says, "You've *earned* the death sentence. This is your wages; this is what's due to you." Sin is so serious to God, Mario, that He's giving you capital punishment. Lying, thieving, blaspheming, fornicating adulterer at heart. Now tell me, what did God do for guilty sinners so we wouldn't have to go to hell? Do you remember?

MARIO: He came up with the idea that, depending on what you do here, you're either good or bad and that's it. You just got to stick to that and have the faith in that.

RAY: No, that's not what He did. Jesus suffered and died on the cross for the sin of the world. The Ten Commandments are called "the moral law." You and I broke the law; Jesus paid the fine. That's what happened on that cross. Mario, if you're in court and someone pays your fine, a judge can let you go. Did you know that? He can say, "Mario, there's a stack of speeding fines here; this is deadly serious, but someone's paid them. You're free to go." And he can do that which is legal and right and just. God loves you so much He became a human being and suffered and died on the cross to take the punishment for the sin of the world. That means you don't have to end up in hell. God can legally forgive your sins because He's the lover of your soul. And then Jesus rose from the dead, defeated death. Mario, if you give up the battle and just say, God, I'm a rebel, and I repent and trust in Christ, God will forgive every sin you've ever committed and grant you everlasting life as a free gift. Do you believe what I'm saying?

MARIO: [tears in his eyes] Yes.

RAY: It's the gospel truth; I wouldn't lie to you. Are you ready to repent and trust in Christ?

MARIO: Yes.

RAY: Can I pray with you?

MARIO: Sure.

RAY: Father, I pray for Mario; thank You we met today. I pray today he'll truly repent and trust in Jesus and have his sins forgiven in a second and pass from death to life. In Jesus's name we pray, amen. You have a Bible at home?

MARIO: No.

RAY: I'm going to give you some literature. Do you know why you're weeping, any idea?

MARIO: Because I've sinned, as a man.

RAY: Ok, that's called "contrition." And the Bible says that godly sorrow, being sorry for your sins, works repentance. So, I trust today that God's brought conviction of sin to you, that you know you've sinned against God and understand that God can forgive you and grant you everlasting life as a free gift. I've got some literature for you. Okay? Mario, thank you for talking to me; I really appreciate it.

MARIO: I appreciate you interviewing me. I do.

This man was humble enough to recognize the authority of God by having remorse for his sins. May we all be like him, mindful of the incredible authority of Jesus, the author of life.

7 | Jesus and His Accusers

There's a reason Jesus had so many accusers. If they could find fault with Him, they could do what contemporary media have done with so many politicians who were thought to be squeaky clean. When the dirt of an extramarital relationship or a very shady deal was publicly exposed, their political careers were over. Jesus's accusers wanted to bring His ministry to a shameful end.

However, even though the accusations against Jesus kept coming, the dirt wouldn't stick. They hated what He said, but they couldn't bring Him down. And there was a reason for that. If the worst things any of us had ever done were publicly known, we would be brought down in a second. But Jesus was no ordinary human being. The Bible tells us that when God was manifest in the flesh (see 1 Tim. 3:16), He was a *sinless* human being (see Heb. 4:15). The lust of the flesh, the lust of the eyes, and the pride of life never manifest in Jesus. His pure eyes never looked at a woman inappropriately, and His perfect humility resisted the sin of pride. Neither could the accuser of the brethren find dirt on the Savior: "I will not speak with you much longer, for the ruler of the world (Satan) is coming. And he has no claim on Me [no power over Me nor anything that he can use against Me]" (John 14:30 AMP).

The sun would sooner turn to ice before the slightest sin could be found clinging to the Savior. Our faith in Him rests on His sinlessness, particularly in that He could not utter a lie—just like His Father: "That by two immutable things, in which it is impossible for God to lie, we might have strong consolation, who have fled for refuge to lay hold of the hope set before us" (Heb. 6:18).

Again, if Jesus sinned even once, Christianity crumbles.

Caught in the Very Act

After the temptation of Jesus in the wilderness, the Bible says that the devil departed from Him "until an opportune time" (Luke 4:13), and the Pharisees were willing and ready vessels when it came to opportune times to accuse Him. When a woman was caught in adultery, they cast her at the feet of Jesus and said, "'Teacher, this woman was caught in adultery, in the very act. Now Moses, in the law, commanded us that such should be stoned. But what do You say?' *This they said, testing Him, that they might have something of which to accuse Him*" (John 8:4–6, emphasis added).

But Jesus turned their accusations back against them. He said:

"He who is without sin among you, let him throw a stone at her first." And again He stooped down and wrote on the ground. Then those who heard it, being convicted by their conscience, went out one by one, beginning with the oldest even to the last. And Jesus was left alone, and the woman standing in the midst. When Jesus had raised Himself up and saw no one but the woman, He said to her, "Woman, where are those accusers of yours? Has no one condemned you?"

She said, "No one, Lord."

And Jesus said to her, "Neither do I condemn you; go and sin no more." (John 8:7–11)

Before we look down on the adulterous woman, we should remember that each of us has been caught in the very act of violating God's law and found ourselves under its terrible wrath. But no one can now accuse us of sin because the moment we trusted Him, Jesus made us clean. We were clothed in His perfect righteousness. Because of such wonderful mercy, we go and sin no more. We sin no more not to *obtain* mercy but *because* of it. And when we do fall into sin—if our eye wanders where it shouldn't or we listen to gossip or we say something we regret—we confess our sins to God, and "He is faithful and just to forgive us our sins and to cleanse us from all unrighteousness" (1 John 1:9).

Give Me a Sign

In Matthew 16, the Pharisees came to Jesus and asked Him for a sign. This request sounds reasonable. If Jesus was the promised Messiah, He could give them some miracle or sign that would convince them once and for all. But their questions weren't sincere:

> Then the Pharisees and Sadducees came, and *testing Him* asked that He would show them a sign from heaven. He answered and said to them, "When it is evening you say, 'It will be fair weather, for the sky is red'; and in the morning, 'It will be foul weather today, for the sky is red and threatening.' Hypocrites! You know how to discern the face of the sky, but you cannot discern the signs of the times. A wicked and adulterous generation seeks after a sign, and no sign shall be given to it except the sign of the prophet Jonah." And He left them and departed. (vv. 1–4, emphasis added)

How often we hear similar requests from skeptics, who ask for "just one sign that God exists," saying that if we can provide that one sign, they will then believe. Their questions and requests are insincere, just as the Pharisees' requests were. The heavens declare His glory, but that isn't enough for skeptics and Pharisees. The invisible things of Him are clearly seen from the creation of the world, but they want more. They don't want to know and love God; they want to test Him endlessly. They don't have humility, and they don't want faith.

Jesus called out the Pharisees' hypocrisy because they came to test Him, and He said they were "a wicked and adulterous generation." However, before He walked away, He gave them knowledge of the greatest sign sinners could ever hope to see. He said, "No sign shall be given to it *except the sign of the prophet Jonah*." Jonah was a foreshadow of the One who would be rejected by men and be tossed over to death—to be swallowed by it for three days and three nights: "For as Jonah was three days and three nights in the belly of the great fish, so will the Son of Man be three days and three nights in the heart of the earth" (Matt. 12:40).

The sign of which Jesus spoke was the gospel. If the world wants an immutable sign of who Jesus is, they need only look to Him who suffered on the cross—to the only One who can save them from sin and death. Then they will know the truth, and the truth will make them free. He will transform them in a moment of time—from loving sin to loving righteousness, born again with a new heart and new desires. God Himself will cause them to walk in His statutes. *That* "sign"—their own personal miracle—will be all they will ever need. But the sign only comes to those who come to Jesus as humble children. It is hidden from proud-hearted, accusing sinners, who seek Jesus only to test Him.

On another occasion, the religious leaders asked Jesus for His thoughts on marriage and divorce:

> The Pharisees also came to Him, *testing Him*, and saying to Him, "Is it lawful for a man to divorce his wife for just any reason?"
>
> And He answered and said to them, "Have you not read that He who made them at the beginning 'made them male and female,' and said, 'For this reason a man shall leave his father and mother and be joined to his wife, and the two shall become one flesh'? So

then, they are no longer two but one flesh. Therefore what God has joined together, let not man separate."

They said to Him, "Why then did Moses command to give a certificate of divorce, and to put her away?"

He said to them, "Moses, because of the hardness of your hearts, permitted you to divorce your wives, but from the beginning it was not so. And I say to you, whoever divorces his wife, except for sexual immorality, and marries another, commits adultery; and whoever marries her who is divorced commits adultery." (Matt. 19:3–9, emphasis added)

The Pharisees milled around Jesus like annoying ants at a picnic. But there is a positive side to these persistent pests. Their insincere question "Is it lawful for a man to divorce his wife for just any reason?" resulted in a verse that gives us our most powerful weapon against the theory of evolution. Jesus simply said, "Have you not read that He who made them at the beginning 'made them male and female'" (v. 4). Case closed. Adam and Eve were not semi-evolved primates. In the beginning they were a *fully formed* male and female with the God-given ability to reproduce after their own kind.

From these accusatory questions, we learn that some of the ordinances given in the Old Testament weren't God's perfect will. They were His *permissive* will. In other words, He allowed certain practices to take place in Israel (such as this certificate of divorce the Pharisees mentioned), but His perfect will frowned upon them.

The Pharisees kept up their questions through Jesus's entire ministry. When they asked Jesus about paying taxes to the occupying Roman authorities, they did so with a wicked and hypocritical motive:

Then the Pharisees went and plotted how they might entangle Him in His talk. And they sent to Him their disciples with the Herodians,

saying, "Teacher, we know that You are true, and teach the way of
God in truth; nor do You care about anyone, for You do not regard
the person of men. Tell us, therefore, what do You think? Is it lawful
to pay taxes to Caesar, or not?"

But Jesus perceived their wickedness, and said, "Why do you
test Me, you hypocrites? Show Me the tax money."

So they brought Him a denarius.

And He said to them, "Whose image and inscription is this?"

They said to Him, "Caesar's."

And He said to them, "Render therefore to Caesar the things
that are Caesar's, and to God the things that are God's." When
they had heard these words, they marveled, and left Him and went
their way. (Matt. 22:15–22, emphasis added)

These skeptical Pharisees couldn't outwit Jesus. Instead, they
marveled and went their way. Such an encounter may have eventually brought some of them to the foot of the cross. They had come
to test Him and trap Him with questions, but they left holding
within their hands the precious seed of life. Jesus was generous,
even to His accusers.

More Accusations

We frequently see in Scripture, "One of them, a lawyer, asked
Him a question, *testing Him*" (Matt. 22:35–36, emphasis added).
Or "Behold, a certain lawyer stood up and *tested Him*" (Luke
10:25, emphasis added). And, "As He said these things to them,
the scribes and the Pharisees began to assail Him vehemently, and
to cross-examine Him about many things; lying in wait for Him,
and seeking to catch Him in something He might say, *that they
might accuse Him*" (Luke 11:53–54, emphasis added).

If we are living godly lives, we are going to be accused also (see
2 Tim. 3:12). Jesus said that the world will hate us as they hated
Him. In other words, the pests of this world will want to spoil
your picnic because they think you are out to spoil theirs:

> If the world hates you, you know that it hated Me before it hated
> you. If you were of the world, the world would love its own. Yet
> because you are not of the world, but I chose you out of the world,
> therefore the world hates you. Remember the word that I said to
> you, "A servant is not greater than his master." If they persecuted
> Me, they will also persecute you. If they kept My word, they will
> keep yours also. But all these things they will do to you for My
> name's sake, because they do not know Him who sent Me. (John
> 15:18–21)

The same devil that accused Jesus of sin, will "day and night"
accuse you: "Then I heard a loud voice saying in heaven, 'Now
salvation, and strength, and the kingdom of our God, and the
power of His Christ have come, for the accuser of our brethren,
who accused them before our God day and night, has been cast
down'" (Rev. 12:10).

We're going to be accused and tempted. The skeptics and
Pharisees of the world will try to pick fights with us. So what
are we supposed to do, especially when it comes to the devil, the
biggest accuser of all? I'd suggest avoiding fights if you can. Let
me illustrate. Early in October 2020, I was at Huntington Beach
in Southern California to do some filming for our television program. I would often take my dog, Sam, with me because he looks
cute in sunglasses, which meant that strangers would stop and
would often agree to go on camera. Dog lovers have an instant
canine camaraderie. In between takes one day, a woman came
close to Sam with her large dog. Sam is the friendliest, sweetest,
and most loving dog you'll ever meet. But now and then, when
another dog gets too close, he can turn from Dr. Jekyll to Mr.
Hyde in a second. It may be that because of his small size he feels
intimidated by larger dogs . . . and this lady's large dog was way
too close.

I politely asked her if she would move her dog back, but instead
of doing so, she smiled and said, "It's okay. My dog is friendly."

It was clear that she thought my dog was so cute he couldn't possibly be aggressive. I replied, "I'm not talking about your dog. I'm talking about mine. He will start a fight." Again, she just smiled and said that her dog was *really* friendly. I wanted to say, "Ma'am, if my dog starts a fight and bites your dog, your dog will instinctively bite back. If a vicious fight begins, because your dog is three times the size of mine, he will probably kill Sam. So, because I love him, I'm going to grab a microphone stand and hit your dog on the head, which will cause serious harm to him. It's at that point in time you'll probably say to yourself, 'Oh, how I wish I had listened to this man and kept the dogs apart.'" Fortunately it didn't come to that. She pulled back on his leash after my third suggestion that the dogs be separated.

Try to avoid a fight with the devil. Simply tell him to get behind you, as Jesus did, because you are busy doing your Father's business. You don't want to have anything to do with him because you know that he came to kill, steal, and destroy (see John 10:10). He was once bigger than you, but now things are different: "You are of God, little children, and have overcome them, because He who is in you is greater than he who is in the world" (1 John 4:4).

If the devil comes close and tries to make you doubt the integrity of God, tempts you to sin, or accuses you night and day, resist him and remain steadfast in the faith. Do what Jesus did when the enemy tried to get Him to kill Himself. He took the two-edged sword of God's Word and hit the devil in the head with it.

> The devil took Him up on an exceedingly high mountain, and showed Him all the kingdoms of the world and their glory. And he said to Him, "All these things I will give You if You will fall down and worship me."
>
> Then Jesus said to him, "Away with you, Satan! For it is written, 'You shall worship the LORD your God, and Him only you shall serve.'"

Then the devil left Him, and behold, angels came and ministered to Him. (Matt. 4:8–11)

We need not contend with the devil, the greatest of all the accusers. The battle against him was won at the cross.

Witnessing Encounter

Accusations take all shapes and sizes. When I thought I was beyond being shocked, a young man named Thomas surprised me with what he unashamedly said about adultery.

RAY: Your name is Thomas?

THOMAS: Yes.

RAY: Does God exist?

THOMAS: He might be out there. But I don't know.

RAY: You can know. See behind me? I've got a bike—an electric bike with a dog on it. Do you believe anyone made the bike?

THOMAS: Yes.

RAY: Why? Why don't you doubt it?

THOMAS: I believe someone made the bike.

RAY: It's got design—wheels and handlebars. The whole of life has got design from the atom to the universe. Does that make sense?

THOMAS: Yes.

RAY: You don't need to be a doubting Thomas anymore. You can *know* God exists. Do you believe the Bible?

THOMAS: Yes. I have an *Action Bible*. It's like a Bible for kids so they can understand it.

RAY: Do you understand it?

THOMAS: Not really.

RAY: Do you know what the message of the Bible is?

THOMAS: No.

RAY: In the Old Testament God promised to destroy a man's greatest enemy—death. And the New Testament tells us how He did it. Let me ask you a few questions, and this will help you understand the gospel. Do you think you're a good person, Thomas? How many lies have you told in your life?

THOMAS: Over a million.

RAY: Have you ever stolen something?

THOMAS: Yes.

RAY: You're a lying thief?

THOMAS: Yes.

RAY: Have you ever used God's name in vain?

THOMAS: Yes.

RAY: Would you ever use your mother's name as a cuss word?

THOMAS: Yes. I don't like my mom. I don't like my father either.

RAY: Do you know what the fifth commandment is?

THOMAS: No.

RAY: "Honor your father and your mother that your days may be long upon the earth and that all may be well with you."[1] We are commanded to honor our parents not because we like them but because God *commanded* us to honor them. Here's another commandment. You shall not commit adultery. Do you know what adultery is?

THOMAS: No.

RAY: That's when a man has sex with another man's wife.

THOMAS: That's when you're a player. You're really doing it when that happens. You're a boss man.

RAY: No. That's called "stupid" when you have sex with another man's wife. Because when he finds out, he's going to kill you. Listen to what Jesus said. He said, "Whoever looks at a woman to lust for her has already committed adultery with her in his heart."[2] When did you last look at pornography?

THOMAS: Last night.

RAY: That's lust. Thomas, I'm not judging you, but you told me you're a liar, a thief, a blasphemer, and an adulterer at heart. So if God judges you by the Ten Commandments on judgment day, are you going to be innocent or guilty?

THOMAS: Guilty.

RAY: Where would you go?

THOMAS: Heaven.

RAY: No. The Bible says that all liars will have their part in the lake of fire.

THOMAS: I will ask for forgiveness. God's the nicest person ever.

RAY: You have just broken the first of the Ten Commandments.

THOMAS: Oh my. I broke another one?

RAY: Yes. He says, "You shall have no other gods before Me."[3] In other words, don't make up a god to suit yourself—that God is the nicest person ever, that He forgives everyone. No, the Bible says His wrath abides on you. You're a child of wrath, and every time you sin, you store up His anger, which is going to be revealed on the day of judgment. So can you see that you're in big trouble?

THOMAS: Yes. Yes.

RAY: What did God do for guilty sinners so that we wouldn't have to go to hell?

THOMAS: He died.

RAY: He died on the cross. Do you understand the legal implications of that?

THOMAS: No.

RAY: You and I broke God's law, the Ten Commandments; Jesus paid the fine. If you're in court and someone pays your fine, a judge can let you go and can do that which is legal and right and just. And God can legally forgive your sins because Jesus paid the fine in His life's blood.

THOMAS: Could I die on a cross and be the next god?

RAY: No, because you're full of sin. Jesus was sinless. He was without sin.

THOMAS: So in His whole life He never did anything wrong?

RAY: Absolutely nothing. The Bible says He was God in human form. God was manifest in the flesh.

THOMAS: Are you telling me He never had sex?

RAY: He never even looked lustfully. He never lied or stole or blasphemed. Let me try and explain it like this, Thomas. If you go before a judge and say, "I want to pay my friend's fine because he's broken the law. I've got some drug money here," is he going to accept the drug money?

THOMAS: No.

RAY: He wants clean money. And God wouldn't accept a tainted sacrifice. It had to be a perfect sacrifice, a perfect payment. And Jesus was the perfect sacrifice. The Bible says, "God commanded his love toward us, in that, while we were yet sinners, Christ died for us," and then He rose again on the third day.[4] If you will simply repent and trust in Jesus, God promises He will forgive your sins and grant you everlasting life. This is your life, and I love you and care about where you spend eternity. So I want you to think seriously about this. Is this making sense?

THOMAS: Yes sir.

RAY: Are you going to think about what we talked about?

THOMAS: Yes sir.

Just remember, no matter how wild the question or strange the response, Jesus has already given a perfect answer to any accuser—past, present, or future. You're stepping out to speak the truth in His name. The world will accuse you, yes, but He has overcome the world.

8 | Jesus and the Greatest Sermon

At the beginning of chapter 2, "Jesus and Hope," we talked about the Sermon on the Mount. Let's backtrack a little bit to go into more detail. I have to tell you, when I love something, I can't stop talking about it. And I just can't get enough of this sermon. I want to walk through the beginning again with you, so we can sit together at the feet of the Master and learn how to start when we speak the truth. When the greatest of all teachers began the greatest of all sermons, He focused on the greatest of all truths. He said, "Blessed are the poor in spirit, for theirs is the kingdom of heaven" (Matt. 5:3).

We are all poor in spirit. We can't do anything for ourselves when it comes to our salvation. When we realize that we are poor in spirit, we are ready for salvation by grace alone. Eternal life comes to us unmerited, and without this foundation there can be no redemption. Jesus spoke of the poor in spirit as being blessed, but we're not blessed *because* we are poor in spirit. The law of God reveals our moral bankruptcy and strips us of any thought of our own worthiness. Being poor in spirit isn't a virtue we possess. It is a revelation that we possess nothing—"Nothing in my hand I bring, simply to Thy cross I cling."[1] Charles Spurgeon said, "A ladder, if it is to be of any use, must have its first step near the ground, or feeble climbers will never be able to mount. It would have been a grievous discouragement to struggling faith if the first blessing had been given to the pure in heart—to that excellence the young beginner makes no claim—while to poverty of spirit he can reach without going beyond his line!"[2] The revelation "I am poor in spirit" is absolutely within reach for a sinner with any shred of humility.

The kingdom of Heaven is gifted by the grace of God to the poor in spirit. It is *freely* given because we have nothing to offer, and most importantly, we can *do* nothing to save ourselves. Our new life in Christ is similar to our old life in Adam in that it comes to us by the grace of God. We think that we are the owners of our eyes, ears, lungs, brains, bones, blood, and hearts. But becoming blind or losing our hearing or getting heart disease shows us how much control we really have over our bodies—that is, very little control. We often speak of a gifted athlete who runs like a gazelle, or a gifted concert pianist whose hands move quickly over the keys in defiance of the eye. Proud hearts think they own their talents, but the humble thank the talent giver. In truth, we don't own anything. Time shows us that. Age slowly takes our youth, our vitality, and our talents.

God owns all things. He possesses the entire animal kingdom, the clouds, the wind, the rain and sunshine, the trees, the flowers, and our bodies and souls: "The earth is the Lord's, and all its fullness. The world and those who dwell therein" (Ps. 24:1).

The realization that everything belongs to God should bring us to a place of heart humility. This is because a humble heart goes hand in hand with the blessed state of being poor in spirit: "Blessed [spiritually prosperous, happy, to be admired] are the poor in spirit [those devoid of spiritual arrogance, those who regard themselves as insignificant], for theirs is the kingdom of heaven [both now and forever]" (Matt. 5:3 AMP).

To the humble, God gives His grace (see James 4:6). Jesus began His sermon with this truth, and this truth marks the beginning of any believer's walk with Jesus. Our spiritual poverty is our wealth.

It is the good soil in which the seed of the Word of God finds root. The Gospels tell us of a certain Roman centurion whom the Jews said was worthy of the attention of the Savior because he had built them a synagogue. They spoke of his good works as giving him merit. But when the centurion himself sent word to Jesus, he said the opposite—that he wasn't worthy:

> And a certain centurion's servant, who was dear unto him, was sick, and ready to die. And when he heard of Jesus, he sent unto him the elders of the Jews, beseeching him that he would come and heal his servant. And when they came to Jesus, they besought him instantly, saying, *That he was worthy for whom he should do this*: For he loveth our nation, and he hath built us a synagogue. Then Jesus went with them. And when he was now not far from the house, the centurion sent friends to him, saying unto him, Lord, trouble not thyself: *for I am not worthy* that thou shouldest enter under my roof: Wherefore *neither thought I myself worthy* to come unto thee: but say in a word, and my servant shall be healed. (Luke 7:2–7 KJV, emphasis added)

While others saw the centurion's works, he knew of his own moral poverty, and it was that which made him rich. His lack qualified him for mercy. That's why we must imitate Jesus and use the moral law to strip the self-righteous naked in their shame before God. We must start at the beginning—with poverty of spirit.

Notice the words Jesus used. He said, "Blessed *are* the poor in spirit, for theirs *is* the kingdom of heaven." We are not *going* to be given the kingdom of Heaven; it's ours now. It's the Father's good pleasure to *give* us the kingdom (see Luke 12:32). Salvation comes to us as a gift the moment we are born again. Someone who is named in a will is its benefactor. Its riches are his. It's signed and sealed. If the ungodly knew what we have in Jesus, they would grasp the gospel with both hands. But they don't. And there's a reason for that—it's because they lack understanding.

A friend once asked me to make a short video encouraging his teenage son. After I sent the clip, he sent me a very nice and sincere thank-you text. Rather than send words, I replied with what I thought was the thumbs-up emoji. It wasn't. It was the thumbs down. Instead of saying that it was a pleasure, that tiny icon instead said, "I hated doing the video and don't bother me ever again with such frivolous requests." I immediately texted "Oops!" and quickly sent the thumbs up, adding, "I'm sure wars have been started because of fat fingers while texting." He sent a laughing emoji and agreed.

Misunderstanding is the devil's playground. When it comes to the most important of issues, the ungodly are blinded by the god of this world: "But even if our gospel is veiled, it is veiled to those who are perishing, whose minds the god of this age has blinded, who do not believe, lest the light of the gospel of the glory of Christ, who is the image of God, should shine on them" (2 Cor. 4:3–4). The ungodly, at the behest of the devil, misinterpret God's signs all the time.

There are two small but very meaningful words that Jesus spoke in the parable of the sower when He gave its interpretation:

> Now the parable is this: The seed is the word of God. Those by the wayside are the ones who hear; then the devil comes and takes away the word out of their hearts, lest they should believe and be saved. But the ones on the rock are those who, when they hear, receive the word with joy; and these have no root, who believe for a while and in time of temptation fall away. Now the ones that fell among thorns are those who, when they have heard, go out and are choked with cares, riches, and pleasures of life, and bring no fruit to maturity. But the ones that fell on the good ground are those who, having heard the word with a noble and good heart, *keep it* and bear fruit with patience. (Luke 8:11–15, emphasis added)

The two tiny but consequential words are "keep it" (v. 15). When the poor in spirit hear the gospel, they understand it and embrace it as a drowning man desperately grabs the hand of someone trying to save him. Why? Because their poverty shows them that they need grace *if they want to live.* They then hold on for dear life. That's because they know that their lives depend on their relationship with God. Those who don't see their sin, don't value the Savior. If "it" is the gospel, they don't "keep it" because they don't think they need it! A failure to see the gravity of sin causes many to fall from the grace of God. They fall back (as did the Galatians) into thinking salvation can be earned: "You have become estranged from Christ, you who attempt to be justified by law; you have fallen from grace" (Gal. 5:4).

Grace alone saves, and every other supposed way of salvation is truly disgraceful in the truest sense of the word.

‖‖‖‖‖‖‖‖‖

Let's take the concept of "poor in spirit" to the story of the rich young ruler (see chapter 3). Notice how earnestly he approached Jesus: "Now as He was going out on the road, one came running, knelt before Him, and asked Him, 'Good Teacher, what shall I do that I may inherit eternal life?'" (Mark 10:17).

The rich young ruler ran to Jesus, knelt down, and asked how to be saved from death. He came close to Jesus, yet he walked away from Him. He was so rich he couldn't accept the very first step. He couldn't be poor in spirit. Compare him to the blind man who was so poor he could only survive by begging:

Then it happened, as He was coming near Jericho, that a certain blind man sat by the road begging. And hearing a multitude passing by, he asked what it meant. So they told him that Jesus of Nazareth was passing by. And he cried out, saying, "Jesus, Son of David, have mercy on me!"

Then those who went before warned him that he should be quiet; but he cried out all the more, "Son of David, have mercy on me!"

So Jesus stood still and commanded him to be brought to Him. And when he had come near, He asked him, saying, "What do you want Me to do for you?"

He said, "Lord, that I may receive my sight."

Then Jesus said to him, "Receive your sight; your faith has made you well." And immediately he received his sight, and followed Him, glorifying God. And all the people, when they saw it, gave praise to God. (Luke 18:35–43)

No doubt this blind man sat by the road because its traffic made it more likely for him to be given money or food from those who passed by. On this day he heard the noise of an excited multitude, perhaps the sound of people running or exuberant voices talking about things they had seen. He asked what was happening, and someone told him that Jesus of Nazareth was passing by. In a few seconds He would be gone, possibly never to pass by that way again. Therefore, the blind man cried out with urgency, saying, "Jesus, Son of David, have mercy on me!"

It would seem that this wasn't the first time he had heard about Jesus because he didn't call Him by the name the crowd had given Him—Jesus *of Nazareth*. He called him Jesus, *son of David*. That perhaps shows us that this blind beggar had been given some godly instruction because the Scriptures speak of the coming of Messiah as "the son of David":

> In those days and at that time
> I will cause to grow up to David
> A Branch of righteousness;
> He shall execute judgment and righteousness in the earth.
> (Jer. 33:15)

Hear now, O house of David! Is it a small thing for you to weary men, but will you weary my God also? Therefore the Lord Himself will give you a sign: Behold, the virgin shall conceive and bear a Son, and shall call His name Immanuel. (Isa. 7:13–14)

The Gospels, too, record that Jesus was the "Son of David": "The book of the genealogy of Jesus Christ, the Son of David, the Son of Abraham" (Matt. 1:1).

The power of poverty in spirit is this: you *know* that you need Jesus. The blind man knew this, and he called out to Jesus by His name. The rich young ruler did not know this and was left with nothing but his empty possessions. Better to be born poor and blind and be poor in spirit than to be born rich and have sight and, because of the sin of pride, walk away from Jesus. The rich young ruler, like so many others, took a detour. Yet we see this often when those who refuse to see their sin don't value the Savior. It breaks our hearts to see a man who is dying of thirst in a desert show no interest in water.

Witnessing Encounter

In mid-2020, I came across a man named Rob who realized his poverty before God. It was a sobering moment when he confessed to me that he had committed murder.

ROB: Maybe in the afterlife that, I think, when you do pass away, probably God gives you an opportunity to be somebody else like a bird, dog, a caterpillar.

RAY: Another human being?

ROB: Maybe, maybe not, I guess, from what I probably think, and I want to say, you only get that one chance.

RAY: Okay, now let me just tell you what you've said to me. You've used the word *probably* a couple of times, *maybe* once, and *I guess*. Shouldn't you find out the truth? You can't say, if you're going to jump out of a plane, "I probably need a parachute, maybe, I guess." This is serious business. This is your eternity, so you want to find the truth. So what do you think of what the Bible says?

ROB: I've never read the Bible.

RAY: It's the world's biggest seller of all time.

ROB: Yes, yes, but I've never read the Bible.

RAY: Let me give you a synopsis of what the Bible says: Old Testament, God promised to destroy man's greatest enemy, death; and the New Testament tells us how He did it. Did you know that?

ROB: No.

RAY: Yes, it tells you how death can be nullified. Have you ever heard the saying, "O Death, where *is* your sting"?[3]

ROB: No.

RAY: Yes, it's from the Bible. It actually says Jesus Christ has abolished death. Did you know that?

ROB: No.

RAY: Which is a weird thing to say because everyone still dies, so how could Jesus Christ abolish death?

ROB: Right.

RAY: Are you afraid of death?

ROB: No.

RAY: Everybody is.

ROB: No.

RAY: You're not afraid?

ROB: No.

RAY: Why not?

ROB: I mean, you know, people come and go; that's the way life is.

RAY: Yes, but if you were lined up behind people who were stepping off a thousand-foot cliff, you lean out and there's 200 to go, and then there's 100, and then there's 10.

Wouldn't you say, "Any way I can get out of this line?" Because you seem like you're accepting the fact you're going to die, and you're not going to do anything about it if you accept it.

ROB: No, no, of course.

RAY: You're just going to wait for your turn.

ROB: Yes.

RAY: When is it?

ROB: Whenever it's . . . I mean everybody's, uh, it's, it's, uh, destined, you know what I mean. It's destined to be like . . .

RAY: You can't do anything about it.

ROB: No.

RAY: So if you're on a highway and there's an 18-wheeler heading for you at 60 miles an hour, you wouldn't bother getting out of the way? You just say, "Oh, it's destined"?

ROB: I mean come on that's, that's different though.

RAY: No, it's not. There's a vehicle, an 18-wheeler called death, with your name on it, and you should be saying, "How can I get out of the way?" because there is a way you can get out of the way. Did you know that?

ROB: Well, yes, you can move of course.

RAY: Well, you can move away from death. I don't just mean the 18-wheeler; I mean death itself, the grim reaper that's going to reap you, and rip you from your family. Man, don't you love your family?

ROB: Of course.

RAY: There's something in you that says, "I don't want to die . . . I want to live."

ROB: Yes, yes.

RAY: It's God-given, that will to live, so I want you to listen to it and don't say there's nothing you can do about it. Say,

I wonder if there's something that can be done about it. Let me tell you what the Bible says causes death. Do you know what causes death?

ROB: No.

RAY: Wages. Death is wages. The Bible says, "The wages of sin is death."⁴ Sin is so serious God's going to pay you in death for your sins. It's like a judge in a court of law who has a criminal in front of him who's committed rape and then killed the three girls that he raped, slit their throats. The judge says to him, "You've earned the death sentence; this is your wages; this is what's due to you." And sin is so serious to God He's given us the death sentence; we're on death row, capital punishment. The soul that sins, it shall die. Do you think you're worthy of the death sentence?

ROB: No.

RAY: Your sin is that bad that God should put you to death?

ROB: No.

RAY: Of course not, you know why? You believe it because you're judging yourself by man's standard, which we all do. God's standard is perfection and holiness, so let's look at the Ten Commandments and see. Have you ever seen those speedometers on the side of the road—they're large and they tell you how fast you're going?

ROB: Yes.

RAY: You know why they do that?

ROB: Well, yes, to have order.

RAY: Yes, to have order, but they want to tell you how much you're transgressing the law so you'll slow down. So I'm going to give you a speedometer; it's the Ten Commandments. Do you think you've kept the Ten Commandments?

ROB: I've broken them.

RAY: Which ones have you broken?

ROB: All of them.

RAY: Really?

ROB: Yes.

RAY: You've murdered somebody?

ROB: Yes.

RAY: Okay, we'll go through them. Is God first in your life? Do you love God with heart, mind, soul, and strength?

ROB: Of course.

RAY: Okay, the second is you should not make yourself a graven image, that means to make sure your concept of God is correct. Go to the third. Have you ever used God's name in vain?

ROB: All the time.

RAY: Would you use your mother's name as a cuss word?

ROB: I say son of a [female dog].

RAY: Calling your mother a dog is not honoring, so that's breaking the fifth commandment, honor your father and mother. If you used your mother's name as a cuss word, you'd be terribly disrespecting her, to substitute your mother's name for a filthy word to express disgust. It'd be a horrible thing to do. But you've taken the name of the God who gave you life, who gave you children, who gave you eyes to see and ears to hear and taste buds to enjoy good food. He lavished His kindness on you, and you took His holy name and used it in the place of a filthy word to express disgust. That's called blasphemy and is so serious it's punishable by death. So I'm going to go back to the first question I asked, if you love God with heart, mind, soul, and strength. You said yes, but it's evident you don't because you've used His name as a cuss word.

ROB: Right.

RAY: Jesus said if you look at a woman and lust for her, you commit adultery with her in your heart. Have you ever looked at a woman with lust?

ROB: No.

RAY: You've never looked at a woman with sexual desire?

ROB: I was always interested in just money, making money.

RAY: Did you have sex before marriage?

ROB: Of course.

RAY: Did you look with lust at your girlfriend?

ROB: It was just how it had to be, you know; I mean it's like we were just young, I guess.

RAY: So, Rob, I'm not judging you, but you've just told me you're a lying, thieving, blasphemous, fornicating adulterer at heart, and you have to face God on judgment day.

ROB: Don't forget murderer.

RAY: And murderer. Are you serious about that?

ROB: Oh yes.

RAY: Wow. So if God judges you by the Ten Commandments on judgment day, are you going to be innocent or guilty?

ROB: Guilty, of course.

RAY: Heaven or hell?

ROB: I would say hell.

RAY: Now does that concern you?

ROB: No.

RAY: Man, it horrifies me!

ROB: Why?

RAY: Rob, I love you; I care about you.

ROB: I care about you and everybody else as well, but I mean, stuff happens. You know what I mean?

RAY: You're in terrible danger. I'd rather fall on the face of the sun than fall into the hands of the living God. So,

man, think about this; this is serious. You can keep your
wife and kids if you get right with God—you can have
them for eternity, you can lead them into the knowledge of
everlasting life. But at the moment, you're the blind leading the blind, so this isn't just you I'm talking about . . .
this is your precious family. Now tell me, what did God
do for guilty sinners so we wouldn't have to go to hell? Do
you know?

ROB: No . . . give up His life?

RAY: Jesus died on the cross. Do you remember His last
words on the cross? "It is finished."[5]

ROB: It is finished; that's what He said?

RAY: Yes, it's finished, saying the debt has been paid. He
came to suffer for sin—the debt has been paid. You and
I broke God's law (the Ten Commandments); Jesus paid
the fine on the cross. That's why He said, "It is finished."
If you're in court and someone pays your fine, a judge can
let you go and do that which is right and just. He can say,
"Rob, there's a stack of speeding fines here. This is deadly
serious, but someone's paid them. You're free to go," and
he can do that which is right and legal. God can legally let
you go. He can let you live forever, legally, because Jesus
paid the fine in full. He can take the death sentence off you
because He's rich in mercy and is kind, despite our sins.
And then Jesus rose from the dead after He suffered for us.
The Bible says whoever repents and trusts alone in Him,
God will grant everlasting life to as a free gift. You don't
have to get religious. You can't earn eternal life; it's a free
gift of God. Ever heard the song "Amazing Grace"?

ROB: Yes.

RAY: Grace means God's unmerited favor: "Amazing grace,
how sweet the sound, that saved a wretch like me. I once
was lost, but now I'm found, was blind but now I see."[6]

The minute you repent and trust Christ, God will open the eyes of your understanding; you'll come out of darkness and to light, out of death and to life. He will make you a brand-new person on the inside so that you love God and so that you love righteousness.

ROB: So you're saying if I change and I repent, I'll be okay?

RAY: You put your faith in Jesus and you've got God's promise He'll forgive every secret sin you've ever committed.

ROB: We'll see. I'm going to do that and we'll see.

RAY: May I pray with you?

ROB: Oh yes, of course.

RAY: Father, I pray for Rob that this day he'll think seriously about his sins and find a place of genuine sorrow, that he'll understand what happened on that cross and put his faith in Jesus as Lord and Savior and pass from death to life because of Your kindness. In Jesus's name we pray, amen.

ROB: Amen.

RAY: I'm going to give you some literature that will help you. Hey Rob, thank you for listening to me and thank you for your honesty. I really appreciate it. Thank you.

This man realized that he had no merit before God—just like all the rest of us. We see this in sharp relief when we place ourselves against the heavenly standard of God's law. Our only hope—our only chance—is to listen to the greatest teacher of all time. To come to Him humbly and say, "I am poor in spirit—I have nothing to offer." To say with the blind man, "Son of David, have mercy on me!"

9 | Jesus and the Lost

When a friend of mine won a gold medal for weight lifting in the 1974 Commonwealth Games, he was already famous because of an incident *before* the final contest. When the weights became too heavy, he dramatically staggered forward and dropped them just a few feet in front of a row of terrified spectators.

Sometime later, the same friend dropped a series of heavy tapes on the parable of the sower in front of me. The teacher on the tapes was Pastor Al Martin, and his teachings were inordinately methodical and repetitive. He went over important points again and again. His repetition engrained biblical truths in me that have lasted a lifetime. It's been well said that repetition is the mother of all learning.

Repetition is also the key to effective advertising. Experts tell us that consistency in presenting a particular brand can increase revenue by an average of nearly 25 percent and that audiences need to see a product as many as seven times before they see its value and go out to buy it.

The point is that if we want to teach an important subject, we should do what Jesus did in Luke 15: He gave a threefold parable in which He repeated the same lesson in three different contexts.

Scripture tells us that sinful men and women were attracted to the Savior like moths to light—and they came to Him because they wanted to hear what He had to say: "Then all the tax collectors and the sinners drew near to Him to hear Him. And the Pharisees and scribes complained, saying, 'This Man receives sinners and eats with them'" (vv. 1–2).

Rather than be happy that so many were coming to Jesus to sit at His feet and learn, the Pharisees and the scribes stood back and were critical of His lowlife audience. Jesus didn't rebuke them with strong words, as we see Him do at other times. Instead, He gave them a very important lesson:

> Then one of the Pharisees asked Him to eat with him. And He went to the Pharisee's house, and sat down to eat. And behold, a woman in the city who was a sinner, when she knew that Jesus sat at the table in the Pharisee's house, brought an alabaster flask of fragrant oil, and stood at His feet behind Him weeping; and she began to wash His feet with her tears, and wiped them with the hair of her head; and she kissed His feet and anointed them with the fragrant oil. Now when the Pharisee who had invited Him saw this, he spoke to himself, saying, "This Man, if He were a prophet, would know who and what manner of woman this is who is touching Him, for she is a sinner."
>
> And Jesus answered and said to him, "Simon, I have something to say to you."
>
> So he said, "Teacher, say it."
>
> "There was a certain creditor who had two debtors. One owed five hundred denarii, and the other fifty. And when they had nothing with which to repay, he freely forgave them both. Tell Me, therefore, which of them will love him more?"
>
> Simon answered and said, "I suppose the one whom he forgave more."
>
> And He said to him, "You have rightly judged." Then He turned to the woman and said to Simon, "Do you see this woman? I entered your house; you gave Me no water for My feet, but she has washed My feet with her tears and wiped them with the hair of her head. You gave Me no kiss, but this woman has not ceased to kiss My feet since the time I came in. You did not anoint My

head with oil, but this woman has anointed My feet with fragrant oil. Therefore I say to you, her sins, which are many, are forgiven, for she loved much. But to whom little is forgiven, the same loves little." (Luke 7:36–47)

Perhaps He didn't rebuke the Pharisees because they looked on the sinful of their generation in the same way that we sometimes look on those we see as the troublesome of our generation. I'm referring to those who have rings through their lips and noses or are covered in tattoos, use illegal drugs, dress strangely or have weird hairstyles, use filthy language, are pro-abortion or pro-homosexual, use blasphemy, abuse alcohol, love violence, look at pornography, don't discipline their kids, listen to demonic music, or fornicate without any sense of shame.

It's so easy to look down a pharisaic nose at these sinful people. It can even be done with an air of respectability. One godly friend was once very concerned that I wanted to put our witnessing clips on certain platforms that didn't have any censorship. He was worried that damage could be done by associating our ministry with them and that what they said could permanently harm our reputation as a conservative, godly ministry. I thanked him for his concern but said he need not worry. I added, "*These* are the people I want to reach. Imagine porn-watchers (there, but for the grace of God go I) stumbling onto one of our witnessing clips among the filth. It would be a light in the darkness. In my mind, I can hear these people giving testimony on how they were so convicted in their sin, that they broke down in tears of contrition."

If our love is as deep as it should be, we will never look on the unsaved with condescension. We must have concern for their eternal salvation. If we look down on them like the Pharisees looked down on the sinners of their generation, we won't care about their eternal destination. But every lost sinner is deeply valued by God, and their lost state should be our greatest concern.

Let's look at the important lesson Jesus gave in His threefold parable about the value of a lost silver coin, a lost sheep, and finally, a lost human being. A silver coin is an inanimate object. It can't think, eat, see, hear, breathe, or reproduce. A sheep has these capabilities and therefore should be of more value because it is a living entity. But a human being not only thinks, eats, sees, hears, breathes, and reproduces; it has also been made in God's image and therefore should be valued far more than a coin or a common sheep. Jesus referred to the value of a human life in Matthew 12 after being accused of violating the Sabbath:

Now when He had departed from there, He went into their synagogue. And behold, there was a man who had a withered hand. And they asked Him, saying, "Is it lawful to heal on the Sabbath?"—that they might accuse Him.

Then He said to them, "What man is there among you who has one sheep, and if it falls into a pit on the Sabbath, will not lay hold of it and lift it out? Of how much more value then is a man than a sheep? Therefore it is lawful to do good on the Sabbath." Then He said to the man, "Stretch out your hand." And he stretched it out, and it was restored as whole as the other. Then the Pharisees went out and plotted against Him, how they might destroy Him. (vv. 9–14, emphasis added)

Here are the first two portions of the threefold parable:

So He spoke this parable to them, saying:

"What man of you, having a hundred sheep, if he loses one of them, does not leave the ninety-nine in the wilderness, and go after the one which is lost until he finds it? And when he has found it, he lays it on his shoulders, rejoicing. And when he comes home, he calls together his friends and neighbors, saying to them, 'Rejoice with me, for I have found my sheep which was lost!' I say to you that likewise there will be more joy in heaven over one sinner who repents than over ninety-nine just persons who need no repentance.

"Or what woman, having ten silver coins, if she loses one coin, does not light a lamp, sweep the house, and search carefully until she finds it? And when she has found it, she calls her friends and neighbors together, saying, 'Rejoice with me, for I have found the piece which I lost!' Likewise, I say to you, there is joy in the presence of the angels of God over one sinner who repents." (Luke 15:3–10)

Jesus began the parable with "What man of you, having a hundred sheep, if he loses one of them, does not leave the ninety-nine in the wilderness, and go after the one which is lost until he finds it?" It is a rhetorical question. In other words, this is what *should* happen with a good shepherd. He not only searches for and finds the lost sheep but also calls together his friends and neighbors, saying to them, "Rejoice with me, for I have found my sheep which was lost!" In our modern culture, neighbors would probably say, "It's great that you found your lost sheep, but what's with this big party?"

Again, in the normal busyness of contemporary society, if I lost one silver coin and had nine left, I may spend some time looking for it. And if I did find it, I would be happy. But I certainly wouldn't call my friends and neighbors over to our house, saying, "Rejoice with me, for I have found the piece which I lost!" Maybe if I had a rich relative leave me a hundred gold coins that I wanted to share with some of my neighbors, it would be worth interrupting their lives to come over. But certainly not to tell them about finding just one lost coin. But finding a lost sheep or a lost coin would mean everything to a person who has much less than we are used to having. Imagine losing one-tenth of all your wealth—the value of your house, your assets, and your bank accounts combined—yikes! That's what Jesus was talking about. That's why it was such a big deal. But the soul of a person is a much, much bigger loss or gain.

This is the essence of what Jesus was saying: *The rejoicing of a person who finds something that was lost will be in direct proportion to the perceived value of the lost object.* That's a very important truth that is well worth repeating: *The joy experienced by someone in finding a lost object will be proportional to its perceived value.* In other words, if the mislaid coin was a dime-a-dozen coin, there would have been no rejoicing. If the sheep was considered to be worthless, tough mutton, the shepherd would have forgotten about it and simply carried on caring for the remaining 99 percent of the flock. Besides, one missing from among one hundred wouldn't matter.

Therefore, it was a *perceived* value. Jesus didn't tell us that the missing coin was made of solid gold and was worth more than the other coins. He didn't say that the missing sheep was a very rare purebred and was of much greater value than the ninety-nine that remained in the flock. Both the coin and the sheep were nothing special in themselves, *and yet they were very highly prized in their owner's eyes.*

Notice what the woman did when she saw that the coin was lost. She didn't merely begin looking for it. Instead, she *lit a lamp*, swept the house, and searched carefully until she found it. And God has given us a brilliant lamp that we can light for those who sit in the shadow of death: "For the commandment is a lamp, and the law a light" (Prov. 6:23).

I have been encouraging the use of that lamp—that is, the law. I have been repeating the same truth for nearly forty years because it is the most important principle any of us can learn in understanding how to reach the lost. Here it is: The good news of someone paying a fine on my behalf will make no sense unless I understand that I have seriously broken a law. In the same way, *the good news of Jesus paying my debt on the cross will make no sense unless I understand that I have broken the Ten Commandments, the moral law.* Please ponder this thought because it is a profound truth.

Many times as I have taken sinners through the commandments, I have listened to them trivialize their transgressions by saying they've only told *little* lies and stolen *little* things. When they do that, I know that they will almost certainly miss the good news of the gospel. If the lamp doesn't give them light, they will stay in the dark. They won't care what Jesus did on the cross; it will go over their heads. I watch them become bored and distracted as I tell them the unspeakably good news that Christ died for sinners. Again, they miss it because they don't see sin as serious lawbreaking, leaving them in danger of hell. The good news of mercy is irrelevant. Why should the gospel be good news if they haven't gravely sinned against God?

That's why we must thoroughly open up the Ten Commandments as Jesus did throughout the Sermon on the Mount. We must show sinners that sin is extremely serious, meriting the death sentence and damnation in hell. That's the biblical key for the lost to understand the gospel. If these thoughts don't take your breath away with a sense of excitement, please read the previous paragraphs again slowly. It will be worth your time.[1]

Notice that the woman in search for the lost coin not only lit a lamp but also *swept the house*. Once again, we see that God has given us that same law to uncover sin. In the wonderful allegory *The Pilgrim's Progress*, we see the sweeping work of the law:

> Then he took him by the hand, and led him into a very large parlor that was full of dust, because never swept; the which after he had reviewed a little while, the Interpreter called for a man to sweep. Now when he began to sweep, the dust began so abundantly to fly about, that Christian had almost therewith been choked. Then said the Interpreter to a Damsel that stood by, bring hither Water, and sprinkle the room; the which when she had done, it was swept and cleansed with pleasure.
>
> Then said Christian, What means this?
>
> The Interpreter answered, This parlor is the heart of a man that was never sanctified by the sweet Grace of the Gospel: The dust is his Original Sin, and inward Corruptions that have defiled the whole man. He that began to sweep at first, is the Law; but she that brought Water, and did sprinkle it, is the Gospel.[2]

A friend once had a bad eye irritation that made him painfully sensitive to light. I suggested that he regularly wash his eyes in a salt solution. It seems ridiculous to rinse tender eyes with harsh salt water, but God (in His wisdom) saw fit to surround our eyes with salty water. If you've ever tasted your own tears, you will know that to be true.

It's wise to imitate God, even when His ways at first don't make sense. How could making sinners feel the pain of guilt be helpful? Surely they need the mercy of the gospel rather than the wrath of the law? But in the same way that washing tender eyes with salty water will heal them, an honest look at sin is the only hope for a sinner. Scripture says:

> What shall we say then? Is the Law sin? Certainly not! On the contrary, if it had not been for the Law, I would not have recognized sin. For I would not have known [for example] about coveting [what belongs to another, and would have had no sense of guilt] if the Law had not [repeatedly] said, "YOU SHALL NOT COVET." But sin, finding an opportunity through the commandment [to express itself] produced in me every kind of coveting and selfish desire. For without the Law sin is dead [the recognition of sin is inactive]. I was once alive without [knowledge of] the Law; but when the commandment came [and I understood its meaning], sin became alive and I died [since the Law sentenced me to death]. (Rom. 7:7–9 AMP)

When we open up the commandments as Jesus did (see Mark 10:17–19), we show the sinner their terrible danger. With the help of God, we illuminate the darkness and prepare the way for the saving power of the gospel. The law is a tutor to bring us to Christ (see Gal. 3:24) because it instructs us and brings the knowledge of our sin, and in doing so, it shows us that we are in need of mercy.

Jesus said of the woman who lost the coin that she lit a lamp, swept the house, and *searched carefully until she found it*. Does the fact that sinners are lost consume your time and thoughts? It did with Jesus. He said this is why He existed on this earth: "For the Son of Man has come to save that which was lost" (Matt. 18:11). Do we regularly leave the necessities and pleasures of daily life to search diligently for what is lost? This woman was *steadfast* in her search to find a mere coin; how much more should we be steadfast to seek lost human beings: "Therefore, my beloved brethren, be steadfast, immovable, always abounding in the work of the Lord, knowing that your labor is not in vain in the Lord" (1 Cor. 15:58).

Our "labor" is a direct reference to the irksome task of evangelism—seeking the lost: "But when He saw the multitudes, He was moved with compassion for them, because they were weary and scattered, like sheep having no shepherd. Then He said to His disciples, 'The harvest truly is plentiful, but the laborers are few. Therefore pray the Lord of the harvest to send out laborers into His harvest'" (Matt. 9:36–38).

This threefold parable that Jesus told wasn't merely about the value of a lost silver coin or a lost sheep. He used both examples to highlight the value of a lost human being. He didn't tell us that there's joy in Heaven when Christians come together to pray, praise, sing, or worship God. He didn't say that the angels rejoice when we put money in the collection plate or do good works or read the Bible. These are all *fruits* of being a Christian. He didn't say that any of these things send the angels into celebration, *but one sinner coming to repentance does!* In Luke 15:10, He repeated this truth: "Likewise, I say to you, there is joy in the presence of the angels of God over one sinner who repents" (see also v. 7).

A lifeguard diligently keeps watch for a desperately waving hand. He is diligent *because* he values human life. If he reads a book, plays with a puppy, or watches a video instead of watching the water, he isn't a lifeguard. He doesn't guard life at all. He is a wicked fake who betrays his honorable profession.

If I call myself a Christian and profess to love God and love my neighbor as myself, I must diligently scour the world for sinners as they drown in their sin. If I don't care about sinners, if I'm not watching the water for desperate hands, I'm a fake who betrays what God has done for me. Shame on me if I'm distracted by other things—no matter how legitimate they may seem.

Keep these thoughts in mind as Jesus now makes His point—with His most wonderful third part to this parable:

Then He said: "A certain man had two sons. And the younger of them said to his father, 'Father, give me the portion of goods that falls to me.' So he divided to them his livelihood. And not many days after, the younger son gathered all together, journeyed to a far country, and there wasted his possessions with prodigal living. But when he had spent all, there arose a severe famine in that land, and he began to be in want. Then he went and joined himself to a citizen of that country, and he sent him into his fields to feed swine. And he would gladly have filled his stomach with the pods that the swine ate, and no one gave him anything.

"But when he came to himself, he said, 'How many of my father's hired servants have bread enough and to spare, and I perish with hunger! I will arise and go to my father, and will say to him, "Father, I have sinned against heaven and before you, and I am no longer worthy to be called your son. Make me like one of your hired servants."'

"And he arose and came to his father. But when he was still a great way off, his father saw him and had compassion, and ran and fell on his neck and kissed him. And the son said to him, 'Father, I have sinned against heaven and in your sight, and am no longer worthy to be called your son.'

"But the father said to his servants, 'Bring out the best robe and put it on him, and put a ring on his hand and sandals on his feet. And bring the fatted calf here and kill it, and let us eat and be merry; for this my son was dead and is alive again; he was lost and is found.' And they began to be merry.

"Now his older son was in the field. And as he came and drew near to the house, he heard music and dancing. So he called one of the servants and asked what these things meant. And he said to him, 'Your brother has come, and because he has received him safe and sound, your father has killed the fatted calf.'

"But he was angry and would not go in. Therefore his father came out and pleaded with him. So he answered and said to his father, 'Lo, these many years I have been serving you; I never transgressed your commandment at any time; and yet you never gave me a young goat, that I might make merry with my friends. But as soon as this son of yours came, who has devoured your livelihood with harlots, you killed the fatted calf for him.'

"And he said to him, 'Son, you are always with me, and all that I have is yours. It was right that we should make merry and be glad, for your brother was dead and is alive again, and was lost and is found.'" (Luke 15:11–32)

Look at the *value* the father placed on his beloved son. The father saw him when he was a great way off! The implication is that he was waiting and watching for him to return. Oh, this is a picture of God our heavenly Father loving us and watching for us to come to our senses and get out of the pigsty of sin. He sees us from a great way off, has compassion, runs to us, falls upon our neck, and kisses us. How could this ever be!

But Jesus left the best part—the cross—out of this story. He spoke of it to Nicodemus in John 3 and often to His disciples. But He didn't mention the cross to the scribes and Pharisees when telling them this parable. There was no real cost paid for the lost coin, other than the woman's time and effort to look for it. Nor was there cost paid for the lost sheep or the lost son.

But in the gospel itself, we see infinite love expressed in the blood of the cross. As sinners, we weren't merely lost. We hadn't simply gone offtrack. Rather, we had horribly rebelled against our maker and at the same time loved and served evil. We truly sinned against Heaven, and the Father couldn't give us a robe of righteousness until a terrible debt was paid. When the horror of the cross is brought into the picture, the cost of the love that God has for us falls in front of us like the weights my friend dropped in front of those terrified spectators.

Witnessing Encounter

I don't want to give the impression that every time I share the gospel it's almost miraculous. Sometimes things don't go as planned. Early in 2021, I received a voice message saying that a workman named Steve was on his way to our house to repair an appliance that wasn't working. I of course prayed for Steve before he arrived.

I put a couple of gift cards and a book on Bible prophecy I had written called *Counting the Days* on the counter in the kitchen. I buy the $5 cards in bulk from a very popular hamburger chain called In-N-Out. I have found that a gift given for no reason can sometimes speak louder than a thousand sermons. I also grabbed a treat for my dog. I didn't want him bothering Steve when he arrived. But when I opened the door to let Steve in, Sam ignored the treat, ran past me, and started barking at Steve. It really wasn't Sam's fault. He was just trying to protect me from a masked man who had come to our door. Steve looked terrified. He stood there for perhaps ten seconds, unable to move, because this fluffy little dog was barking at him. I felt terrible. This had not started well. After I put Sam on a leash, I apologized to Steve and invited him in.

As he was working under the sink, I said that we had chickens and asked him if he would like a dozen fresh eggs. He said thank you but no because he and his wife had just purchased a stack of eggs. Now was my big moment. I took courage and said, "Steve, I've got a question for you. Do you think there is an afterlife?"

He stopped working, turned around, and looked directly at me. "I don't talk about that sort of thing during working hours."

It clearly wasn't about talking during working hours. It was a form of shutting the door. He didn't want to talk about the things of God. So I pulled back the second string of my bow and fired off: "Would you like a free copy of a book that I wrote on the pandemic?"

"No, thank you."

"How about a couple of five-dollar gift cards?"

Sadly, Steve turned those down also. I got the message. He didn't want to talk about God or be given any literature, and if I had a brand-new Lamborghini with a full tank of high-octane gas, he wasn't interested. So for the next ten minutes I showed him as much kindness and verbal love as I could. I was determined that this man wasn't going to leave without knowing that I cared about him. Then I prayed for Steve that God would use somebody else to touch his life. I was disappointed but not at all discouraged because if it had been God's timing for Steve to hear the gospel, it would have happened. Ask Saul of Tarsus about that. He had already taken a detour around the gospel. But God had a different path for him.

10 | Jesus and Atheism

In the last chapter, I spoke about giving Steve a Lamborghini with a full tank of high-octane fuel. Let's imagine for a moment that Lamborghini—the famous Italian car manufacturer known for producing the most luxurious of sports cars—wanted to create good will. So the company randomly chose one young man and gave him a brand-new, state-of-the-art Lamborghini worth over half a million dollars.

They also gave him their manufacturer's manual and told him to study it carefully. The vehicle would run only on a special high-grade fuel. The manual sternly warned that *any* low-grade fuel would have three predictable results: (1) the engine would splutter, (2) it would give off a white, poisonous smoke, and (3) the vehicle would then grind to a halt.

The young man was delighted with the car. However, instead of carefully reading the manual as he had been told to do, he tossed it aside and drove the car until it ran out of gas. He then had the tank filled with a cheap, low-grade fuel.

To his surprise, the vehicle began to splutter, the engine gave off a pungent, white smoke, and the car ground to a halt on the side of the road. It did exactly what the manual warned it would do if low-grade fuel was put into the tank. But instead of blaming himself for putting bad fuel in the tank, he became very angry at both the manufacturer and the manual. In a rage, he peeled the Lamborghini nameplate off the car and threw it and the manual into a ditch on the side of the road. He then became so contemptuous against Lamborghini that he denied they had anything to do with making the vehicle. He said the car made itself.

The story is believable right up until the last six words: "He said the car made itself." Such a conviction isn't rational. Anyone who believed that a car either happened by accident or made itself could be considered mentally ill.

Sam Harris is a well-known atheist who spends much of his time in an indignant rage against God and the Bible. He hates both. This is because he holds God morally responsible for the suffering of humanity. He has the utmost contempt for someone he believes doesn't exist.

The Bible—the maker's manual—warns that the result of sin will predictably be disease, suffering, and death. We certainly see those results, and we do live in the midst of a sinful generation—one that revels in pornography, loves violent entertainment, and incessantly uses blasphemy. It loves adultery, fornication, homosexuality, and it even rejoices in the evil of abortion. In other words, it has chosen the lowest grade of fuels. Consequently, just as the Scriptures warn, it has resulted in terrible diseases and pain, endless suffering, and of course death.

The following quote shows the indignation that Harris has toward the God he hates and the utmost contempt he has for Scripture:

Nine million children die every year before they reach the age of five. Picture an Asian tsunami of the sort we saw in 2004, that killed a quarter of a million people. One of those, every ten days, killing children only under five. That's 24,000 children a day, a thousand an hour, 17 or so a minute. That means before I can get to the end of this sentence, some children would have died in terror and agony. Think of the parents of these children. Think of the fact that most of these men and women believe in God, and are praying at this moment for their children to be spared. And their prayers will not be answered. . . . Any God who would allow children by the millions to suffer and die this way, and their parents to grieve in this way, either can do nothing to help them or doesn't care to. He is therefore impotent or evil.[1]

The pains of humanity are much worse than the horrible picture Harris paints. Suffering and death are not confined to children. Every day, 150,000 human beings die. That's 6,000 every hour and a staggering 54,000,000 every year! And whatever way they die, every single instance of death stands as a stark and sobering reminder that what the maker's manual says is true. We live in a fallen creation, and we have given ourselves to evil and rebellion against God. What we see happening is exactly what the Bible says would happen. Death is the consequence of sin.

Harris believes that because God doesn't come to our aid, He is either impotent or evil. But if He created the universe, He is not impotent. And that leaves Harris with the thought that the universe made itself—which is not only scientifically impossible but also borders on insanity. So for Harris, the only alternative left is that God is evil. He is evil because He is not fulfilling His supposed moral obligation to humanity. However, Scripture gives one more option. The Bible says that God is holy. It tells us that He is pure righteousness, that human beings are pure evil, and that as the judge of the universe His only moral obligation is to see that criminals are punished.

Here is the divine indictment:

> As it is written:
> "There is none righteous, no, not one;
> There is none who understands;
> There is none who seeks after God.
> They have all turned aside;
> They have together become unprofitable;
> There is none who does good, no, not one."

"Their throat is an open tomb;
With their tongues they have practiced deceit";
"The poison of asps is under their lips";
"Whose mouth is full of cursing and bitterness."
"Their feet are swift to shed blood;
Destruction and misery are in their ways;
And the way of peace they have not known."
"There is no fear of God before their eyes." (Rom.
  3:10–18)

It is because of our wickedness that God's righteous wrath abides on every one of us (see John 3:36). Scripture calls us "children of wrath" (see Eph. 2:3). But because Harris refuses to believe the maker's manual, he maintains that the maker is evil and that he himself is both intellectually and morally superior to God. Harris suffers from the ultimate delusion of grandeur.

Again, Harris's beliefs are completely irrational. In saying that there was no maker, he automatically defaults to the scientific impossibility that nothing created everything. But note carefully, he doesn't believe that there was nothing in the beginning. Rather, that *nothing* was the prime mover that created everything. He believes that the beauty of the deep blue sky, the magnificence of tall green trees, the awe-inspiring sight of eagles in flight, and the freshness of the early morning air had no maker. To believe that there's no evidence of a Creator is a trillion times more foolish than to believe that a Lamborghini had no maker. Yet that's what Harris believes—that there is no God. At the same time, Harris believes that the God who he claims doesn't exist should be held accountable for the evil of not being humanity's butler. God should stay quiet when it comes to the issues of *our* moral accountability, but at the same time He should run to the assistance of dying children because He is morally accountable to *us*.

There is another glaring inconsistency in his beliefs. Harris believes that these precious children, the ones for whom he mourns,

150

are nothing but undeveloped primates. And these primates died because of a cold and cruel principle—evolution's survival of the fittest. They perished because they were a weak link in the species. Only the strong survive. Why should Harris, then, complain about their deaths? His worldview can offer no hope for the living or the dying. Life has no purpose, nor is there any ultimate right or wrong.

If there's no ultimate right and wrong, the deaths of children are neither good nor evil. It is no wonder that in the face of such utter hopelessness, this generation faces an epidemic of suicide. Harris preaches a hopeless atheistic futility. At the same time, he has the audacity to turn people against God and the gospel—the only hope that any human being can have both in this life and in their death. And he does it by twisting the truth of Scripture. Listen to what Harris says of God: "He's created this cosmos as a vast laboratory in which to test our powers of credulity. And the test is this: Can you believe in this God on bad evidence? And if you can, you can win an eternity of happiness after you die."[2]

Harris created an easy-to-tear-apart straw man. God did not create this cosmos as a laboratory to test human gullibility. Incidentally, the word *cosmos* means "order, good order, orderly arrangement."[3] Neither did God surround us with bad evidence. Instead, everywhere we look we see "order, good order, orderly arrangement." And in the amazing, ordered arrangement, we see the evidence of His creative hand. *Everything* has order—from the tiny atom to the massive galaxy. It has order because it's been *arranged* that way. Cars don't make themselves. Neither do flowers, birds, trees, fruits, the seasons, the human body, male and female, the sun, the moon, or the stars. These things are only "bad evidence" to a fool, just as the maker's manual says:

> For since the creation of the world His invisible attributes are clearly seen, being understood by the things that are made, even His eternal power and Godhead, so that they are without excuse,

because, although they knew God, they did not glorify Him as God, nor were thankful, but became futile in their thoughts, and their foolish hearts were darkened. Professing to be wise, they became fools. (Rom. 1:20–22)

Remember the words of the psalmist: "The fool has said in his heart, 'There is no God'" (Ps. 14:1).

The foundation for Harris's foolish beliefs is faulty, and the theology he built on top of it is bad. He said that if you believe in God, "you can win an eternity of happiness after you die." Again, he created a flimsy straw man that he could easily pull apart. No one "wins" eternal life. Salvation doesn't come to us because of what we do. That is basic biblical theology. Eternal life comes purely by the grace of God. But Harris doesn't care what the manual says. He asserts instead that belief in God despite "bad evidence" is rewarded with everlasting happiness. That is just not true: "For by grace you have been saved through faith, and that not of yourselves; it is the gift of God, not of works, lest anyone should boast" (Eph. 2:8–9). Atheists, who are famous for assigning responsibility where it doesn't belong, don't understand that we don't "win" anything when it comes to our faith.

The World's Error

Just is perhaps the most misunderstood word when it comes to the nature of God. To be *just* means to be "based on or behaving according to what is morally right and fair."[4] Perhaps that's what Harris believes *just* to mean, but that definition is meaningless without an understanding of "right and fair." Look at how he applies this meaningless definition to God:

We're told that God is loving, and kind, and just, and intrinsically good; but when someone like myself points out the rather obvious and compelling evidence that God is cruel and unjust, because he visits suffering on innocent people, of a scope and scale that would embarrass the most ambitious psychopath, we're told that God is mysterious, ok. "Who can understand God's will?"[5]

Harris wants God to conform to his own definitions—and that's the definition of pride.

Another word that is completely misunderstood in terms of God's nature is *good*. Harris appeals to God as supposedly being "intrinsically good." But the four words he uses—*loving, kind, just,* and *good*—placed alongside one another paint the picture of a benevolent father figure in the minds of those who are ignorant of their biblical meanings. This is clearly Harris's—and the world's—error. The image he sees of God is one of being sweet and nice. How could such a person do nothing in the face of human suffering? But his image is wrong. The "god" he doesn't believe in doesn't exist. Harris is terribly confused because he refuses to believe the testimony of Scripture, the maker's manual.

Let's consider the goodness of God for a moment. If He is good, should He punish evil? The obvious answer is that He must. Any judge who is good must *always* see that justice is done. He *cannot* compromise the law. If the judge does compromise, he's neither good nor just. *Good* does not equal *nice* in criminal justice or in divine judgment. That thought should help to quash the image of God as a celestial Santa Claus.

Look at what God said to Moses about His goodness:

And [Moses] said, "Please, show me Your glory."

Then He said, "*I will make all My goodness pass before you,* and I will proclaim the name of the LORD before you. I will be gracious to whom I will be gracious, and I will have compassion on whom I will have compassion." But He said, "You cannot see My face; for no man shall see Me, and live." And the LORD said, "Here is a place by Me, and you shall stand on the rock. So it shall be, while My glory passes by, that I will put you in the cleft of the rock, and will cover you with My hand while I pass by. Then I will take away My hand, and you shall see My back; but My face shall not be seen." (Exod. 33:18–23, emphasis added)

When Moses asked to see God's glory, God referred to His *goodness*, saying that Moses could not look upon Him and live. But surely goodness is positive and beneficial. How, then, could the goodness kill Moses?

I want to warn you; this next example is quite graphic. Think of a really good judge who loves justice. In front of him stands a man who kidnapped a sweet teenage girl at knifepoint. For months he raped and tortured her. Then he cut her throat, carved up her body, and fed it to his hungry dogs. As the judge listens to the grizzly details, his anger toward the criminal will be in direct proportion to his goodness. If the judge isn't good, he won't be angry with the criminal. But if he is a lover of justice, he will burn with fury and swiftly bring the law down on him to the maximum.

If God is perfectly just and good, He will be equally angry at all who practice evil. And here are the questions that can change our wrong image of God: What does He consider to be "morally right and fair"? What does He consider to be evil? Let's look at something most of us are guilty of doing—lying. Scripture tells us that "lying lips are an abomination to the LORD" (Prov. 12:22). That means that a liar is extremely detestable to God.

The way to tell how angry a good judge is at any criminal is to consider the sentence he gives. If he hands down a ten-dollar fine, the judge didn't consider the crime to be serious. But if he hands down the death sentence, you can be sure that he considers the offense to be very serious. How bad is lying to a holy God? Here is the fearful answer: "All liars shall have their part in the lake which burns with fire and brimstone, which is the second death" (Rev. 21:8).

God is so serious about sin that He's given all of us the death sentence. Death is the arresting officer that will drag us before the judge of the universe to be sentenced for violating His morally perfect law. God will judge every single one of us—that's how good and how just He is. And that's why Moses couldn't stand in His presence and live. Remember, Moses asked to see God's goodness, not His niceness. If God showed Himself to Moses, the goodness of God would have spilled onto him like livid lightning and justly put him to death. The God who Sam Harris thinks is evil is the One he must face on judgment day.

If you let yourself think about it for a minute, I'm sure you'll realize that you've been tempted to accuse God in similar ways as Harris. We must not do this. We must humbly stand before God's goodness. We all need to be hidden in the cleft of the rock. As the song goes:

> Rock of Ages, cleft for me,
> Let me hide myself in Thee;
> Let the water and the blood.
> From Thy riven side which flowed,
> Be of sin the double cure,
> Save me from its guilt and power.
>
> Nothing in my hands I bring,
> Simply to Thy cross I cling;
> Naked, come to Thee for dress,
> Helpless, look to Thee for grace:
> Foul, I to the fountain fly,
> Wash me, Savior, or I die.[6]

The World's Hypocrisy

One might think that it is noble of Sam Harris to have such a sincere concern for the lives of perishing children. However, his—and the world's—hypocrisy is evident in the fact that he not only couldn't care less that millions of babies are slaughtered in the womb through abortion, but he also mocks those who do care:

One of the most pernicious effects of religion is that it tends to divorce morality from the reality of human and animal suffering. Religion allows people to imagine that their concerns are moral when they are not—that is, when they have nothing to do with suffering or its alleviation. Indeed, religion allows people to imagine that their concerns are moral when they are highly immoral—that is, when pressing these concerns inflicts unnecessary and appalling suffering on innocent human beings. This explains why Christians . . . expend more "moral" energy opposing abortion than fighting genocide. It explains why you are more concerned about human embryos than about the lifesaving promise of stem-cell research.[7]

Nowhere in the Gospels do we read of Jesus being challenged by an atheist to provide evidence that there was a Creator. That's because asking for evidence of God is like asking someone at noon on a cloudless day to provide evidence that the sun exists. Historically, atheism has been very rare. It is a *modern* phenomenon—we could call it a modern detour—that has gripped an intellectually bankrupt and godless generation. Sir Isaac Newton said, "Atheism is so senseless. When I look at the solar system, I see the earth at the right distance from the sun to receive the proper amounts of heat and light. This did not happen by chance."[8] The Bible uses an even stronger word to describe atheists. It calls them fools (see Pss. 14:1; 53:1).

Witnessing Encounter

I was on my bike when I rode past three young men. I heard one of them mention I had a dog that was wearing sunglasses, so I turned around and went back. One of them (whose name was Juan) was an atheist.

RAY: What's your thoughts on the afterlife?
ERIC: I believe that there's an afterlife.

JUAN: I do not think so. I come from an all-Christian family, and, it's kind of what I was taught and raised to believe. And also, I just feel like I'd rather believe in something rather than believe in nothing, you know?

SAM: I'm not sure.

RAY: You're not sure?

SAM: Yeah. Not sure.

RAY: You ever think about death?

SAM: No, I try not to. [laughs]

RAY: It's not a pleasant thought, is it?

SAM: Not the best.

RAY: You love life?

SAM: Oh, yeah.

RAY: Are you thankful for it?

SAM: Yes. Very, very thankful.

RAY: Who to?

SAM: Who to? Who am I thankful for?

RAY: What I'm trying to say is, Do you believe in God's existence?

SAM: Oh! Like, yeah.

RAY: Are you thankful to Him for your life?

SAM: Yeah. For sure, yeah.

RAY: [addressing Eric] How is your walk with the Lord? Is it really good, or is it a little lukewarm? Let's say, 10 out of 10, you're really going great with the Lord, 1 out of 10, there's nothing much happening. Where would you be?

ERIC: Uh, to be honest, probably not too strong. I mean, it kind of goes through phases. Sometimes I'm like an 8, sometimes I'm like a 2, because it comes and goes in phases. But I think it's, I lack consistency sometimes, you know?

RAY: Juan, do you believe in God's existence?

JUAN: Uh, no.

RAY: So you think all of this happened by accident: beautiful blue sky, the seasons, the fruits? Flowers, birds, trees, puppies, kittens, everything came from nothing. Is that right?

JUAN: No, I believe it came from somewhere, just not in the fact that there's like an actual Creator.

RAY: A man was really bored with life—he was an ordinary guy, no one knew about him. He robbed a bank, things went wrong, and he killed three people. Is he still an ordinary guy that nobody knows about, or has something happened?

SAM: Something happened, for sure. I mean, he's still the same person, but he killed people, and—

RAY: So what's going to happen to him?

SAM: He's going to go to jail, probably, if he doesn't get away with it.

RAY: So the police are going to hound him because he's done something morally wrong?

SAM: Yeah.

RAY: Why bother about justice? Why not just say, "Oh, the guy killed a few people, who cares? Survival of the fittest"? Why do we care about justice?

SAM: To give people what they deserve, I guess. I don't know.

RAY: To give people what they deserve? That's what justice does?

SAM: I guess.

RAY: That is a really good definition of justice: getting what you deserve. So, what's going to happen to you after you die? Are you going to get what you deserve?

SAM: Probably. [laughs]

RAY: Where are you going to go, Heaven or hell?

SAM: I don't know.

RAY: If you died today, where would you go?

ERIC: Ha, I hope I'd go to Heaven.

RAY: You're not sure?

ERIC: Not 100 percent sure, but I think I would.

RAY: Do you think you're a good person?

ERIC: Yeah, I would say I'm a good person.

SAM: I'm a good person. I'll make it to Heaven.

RAY: You're a morally good person?

SAM: I think so.

RAY: How many lies have you told in your life?

SAM: A lot.

JUAN: Plenty.

ERIC: I don't lie too much, to be honest with you.

RAY: Have you ever stolen something?

SAM: Yeah.

RAY: So you're a lying thief?

SAM: Yeah.

RAY: You still think you're a morally good person?

SAM: Yeah, I do. [laughs]

RAY: Have you ever used God's name in vain?

SAM: Yeah, I have.

RAY: Now, Jesus said, "Whoever looks at a woman to lust for her has already committed adultery with her in his heart."⁹ Have you ever looked at a woman with lust?

SAM: Um, yeah, sure.

JUAN: No, I haven't.

RAY: You haven't?

JUAN: No.

RAY: Are you homosexual?

JUAN: No, I am not.

RAY: When did you last look at pornography?

JUAN: Probably like in the past week.

RAY: So, Sam, I'm not judging you, but you've—this is for you, not for me—

SAM: I'm an adultist. [laughs]

RAY: Well, you're a lying, thieving, blasphemous adulterer at heart.

SAM: That's what it was. [laughs]

RAY: If God judges you by the Ten Commandments on judgment day, are you going to be innocent or guilty?

SAM: I would be innocent, probably.

RAY: Why?

SAM: Just, they're minor. Like, it's just not as big as you think it would be. Like, white lies aren't . . . but sometimes in life you lie just because.

RAY: Do you know what you're doing?

SAM: Huh?

RAY: You're trying to justify yourself; you're trivializing your sins. And yet God says sin is so serious that it's punishable by death—God's given you the death sentence for your sins. It's like that man who shot the three people when he was robbing a bank and saying, "Judge, it was no big deal. They were just ordinary people; this is not serious." The judge would say, "Let me show you how serious it is: we're sending you to the electric chair."

And Juan, you're in debt to the law. You're not just an ordinary guy among billions; you're in debt to God's law. His wrath abides on you, just like the wrath of the law abides on the man who's committed a bank robbery and murdered people. They'll chase and they'll hound him to bring him to justice. The Bible says God will hound you and bring you to justice. He's given you the death sentence already because of your sin. The Bible says that the wages of sin is death; sin is so serious in God's eyes that He's given you the death sentence. You're under capital punishment.

JUAN: We don't know until we actually die, and we, everyone's going to—

RAY: We do. We've got God's Word on it. There's no higher authority. The Bible says if you die in your sins, you'll end up damned, and I don't want that to happen to you. I don't want you to go to hell.

SAM: So I'd better stop lying—

RAY: That won't help you.

SAM: —and looking at women.

RAY: No, that won't help you.

SAM: So what . . . what are you trying . . . then what are you saying?

RAY: I'm trying to say you need God's mercy. God will forgive you and cleanse you and wash away those sins in an instant, because Jesus took the punishment for them on the cross. Did you know that?

SAM: Yeah, I did. But what's the difference between doing all those things wrong, then on your last day, you say, "Oh, okay, let me just go back to God and ask for forgiveness before I die"? And then you die, and you asked for forgiveness before you died, and then you're fine, right?

RAY: No, not right. That'd be a dumb thing to do, because God could kill you just before you—

SAM: Just before you ask for forgiveness. [laughs]

RAY: —just before you asked. You know, He did that with a guy in Genesis chapter 38. He didn't like what a man did sexually, and it says, "and the LORD killed him."[10]

SAM: Yeah.

RAY: So we're talking serious business. Jesus said that if your eye causes you to sin, pluck it out and cast it from you, for it's better to enter Heaven without an eye than to go to hell with both your eyes.

SAM: Whoa!

RAY: Man, your life is so precious! Don't throw it away by serving sin.

JUAN: Why I wasn't scared of death is because I see it as leaving something behind when you die. And then even if you die, if you go to hell, or, you know, wherever the other place is, you would leave something good behind, like kids, family. And then it all depends how the world's going to be at that point, you know. Lots of things are changing.

RAY: Well, you can thank God that you left family behind. God gave you the ability to reproduce after your own kind. He gave you the ability to have sex and enjoy the pleasures of sex. And so, you can have your own children because God gave you that ability. Now what did God do for guilty sinners so we wouldn't have to go to hell, do you know?

JUAN: Based on what the Bible says, kind of, He had to die for everyone's sins.

RAY: You and I broke God's law, the Ten Commandments; Jesus paid the fine. That's why He said, "It is finished," just before He died. In other words, the debt has been paid. Sam, if you're in court and someone pays your fine, even though you're guilty, the judge can let you go because someone else paid the fine, and he can do that which is legal. He can say, "Sam, there's a stack of speeding fines here; this is deadly serious. But someone's paid them, so you're out of here." And he can do that which is legal because someone paid the fine. Well, God can dismiss your case, take death off you, save you from hell, because Jesus paid the fine in His life's blood. Understand that?

SAM: Yes, I get that.

RAY: And He can do that which is legal toward you because Christ paid the fine and fulfilled God's law. And then He rose from the dead, defeated death, and now God offers you everlasting life as a free gift upon your repentance and faith in Jesus.

At the moment, you're serving money, but the Bible says you cannot serve God and mammon. You'll either love one and hate the other, or hate one and love the other. So you either love God or love money. You'll either have faith in God or have faith in money as your future provider.

JUAN: As a human, as basically an animal that we are, we need to survive. And if that's basically the best way to survive out there, you know, survival of the fittest, then that's basically how I take it. You gotta survive in this world that we live in.

RAY: Let me answer that question. At the moment, you're not fit to survive; you're going to die. But God will make you fit to survive by forgiving your sins and granting you everlasting life. And by the way, you're not a beast; you're not a primate; you're not an animal. You're made in the image of God with a sense of right and wrong and a responsibility to Him for your sins. And He's offering you everlasting life as a free gift. Oops, time is going. It's going for all of us, so please think about this. Will you think about what we talked about today?

JUAN: I think of the possibility that everyone might die, you know, at any moment, and at any second. And I'm a firm believer of that.

RAY: Okay, I'm pleased you are, because Jesus spoke of a man that was so rich he built bigger barns to put his goods in, and he said, "I'm going to take it easy from now on." But God said, "You fool, tonight your soul will be required of you, and who will have those things that you have saved?"[11] So it is with whoever is not rich toward God. You've got to think about it with that attitude. Have you got a Bible at home?

ERIC: Uh yeah, I don't read though. I don't read any books.

RAY: Why not?

ERIC: It's too boring. I never sit down and just read, you know.

RAY: A man was very rich. He was on a ship, and the ship began to sink. He had a belt around him filled with gold, a money belt, and it weighed forty pounds, so packed with gold. But when he fell in the water, he wouldn't take it off because he so loved it. So it took him to his death. And sin will do that to you, we so love it. It's so pleasurable. Pornography, fornication, lying and stealing, we love darkness. But it'll take you to hell, so it's not worth it. And the moment you repent and trust in Christ, God will give you a new heart so you'll love righteousness. That's what a Christian is, someone who loves what is right. And that's a miracle for a sin-loving sinner. Is this making sense?

SAM: It does; it makes sense.

RAY: You going to think about what we talked about?

SAM: For sure.

RAY: Do you have a Bible at home?

SAM: I do, but I don't remember the last time it was . . . moved. [laughs]

RAY: Please dust it off. Man, it's God's love letter to you.

SAM: I gotta dust off my Bible. [laughs]

RAY: Yeah, dust it off; it's God's love letter to you. And don't neglect your eternal salvation; there's nothing more important. Seek first the kingdom of God and His righteousness. Everything else will be added to you. Sam, you've been a good sport, and I'll give you some literature. Hey, thanks for listening to me. I really appreciate it.

SAM: Yeah, no worries. It means a lot, thank you.

11 | Jesus and His Hard Sayings

When the religious leaders sent officers to arrest Jesus, they clearly thought His arrest would put an end to their troubles. Crowds couldn't follow Him and hear His teachings if He was under lock and key. These officers were temple guards who were no doubt trained to deal swiftly with troublemakers. And to the scribes and Pharisees, Jesus certainly was a troublemaker worthy of being arrested. But the officers came back empty-handed, astonished, and dumbfounded by His words. They said, "No man ever spoke like this Man!" (John 7:46).

In a lonely and dark world, the words of Jesus are a wonderful guiding light for lost souls. They are sometimes so simple that a child can understand them and yet in other places so profound the most intellectual of scholars still marvel at them. And so they should.

It is impossible for any honest soul not to be deeply impressed by the statements Jesus made, the questions He asked, and the answers He gave. Even great philosophers are merely lost sinners—those who are formulating their own thoughts about the mysteries of life. But nothing was a mystery to Jesus. He spoke with great authority because His words were explanatory truth. The greatest men in history who studied the New Testament in any depth couldn't help but be impressed by His person:

> I am a Jew, but I am enthralled by the luminous figure of the Nazarene. . . . No man can read the gospels without feeling the actual presence of Jesus. His personality pulsates in every word. No myth is filled with such life.
>
> Albert Einstein, scientist and mathematician[1]

> I know men and I tell you that Jesus Christ is no mere man. Between Him and every other person in the world there is no possible term of comparison. Alexander, Caesar, Charlemagne, and myself founded empires; but [on] what foundation did we rest the creations of our genius? Upon force. Jesus Christ founded an empire upon love; and at this hour millions of men would die for Him.
>
> Napoleon Bonaparte, French general, politician, and emperor[2]

> For thirty-five years of my life I was, in the proper acceptation of the word, nihilist, a man who believed in nothing. Five years ago my faith came to me. I believed in the doctrine of Jesus Christ and my whole life underwent a sudden transformation. Life and death ceased to be evil. Instead of despair, I tasted joy and happiness that death could not take away.
>
> Leo Tolstoy, Russian author of *War and Peace*[3]

> It is a very good thing that you read the Bible. . . . The Bible is Christ, for the Old Testament leads up to this culminating point . . . Christ alone. . . . He lived serenely, as a greater artist than all other artists, despising marble and clay as well as color, working in living flesh.
>
> Vincent van Gogh, artist[4]

Had the doctrines of Jesus been preached always as pure as they came from his lips, the whole civilized world would now have been Christian.

Thomas Jefferson, third president of the United States[5]

Because of who Jesus is, nothing He said should be discarded as superficial or meaningless. Rather, every word He spoke should be scrutinized with a sincere and humble hunger to understand its meaning. In this chapter, we are going to look at the hard sayings of Jesus. But let's remember how marvelous His words are. He owns all mysteries. We must walk on this holy ground knowing that we are poor in spirit and that we cannot know anything without Him. It is with that sense of humility that we approach some of the most difficult things Jesus said.

In Matthew 8:22 Jesus said that the dead should bury the dead. Isn't that disrespectful? Let's look at the context:

And when Jesus saw great multitudes about Him, He gave a command to depart to the other side. Then a certain scribe came and said to Him, "Teacher, I will follow You wherever You go."

And Jesus said to him, "Foxes have holes and birds of the air have nests, but the Son of Man has nowhere to lay His head."

Then another of His disciples said to Him, "Lord, let me first go and bury my father."

But Jesus said to him, "Follow Me, and let the dead bury their own dead." (Matt. 8:18–22)

When a scribe said that he would follow Jesus wherever He went, Jesus answered him and, at the same time, shot down the erroneous prosperity gospel—"The Son of Man has nowhere to lay His head." In other words, "Don't follow Me because of all the nice things you think you'll get." Prosperity preachers preach that the prodigal should return to his father to get a ring and a robe and to feast on the fatted calf. Rather than coming because he has sinned against Heaven and desires to *be* a servant, he comes home to have his father serve *him*. The scribe was that kind of greedy prodigal, and Jesus knew it. The prosperity gospel is a gospel of greed that produces nothing but false converts.

When a disciple said, "Lord, let me first go and bury my father," Jesus replied, "Let the dead bury their own dead," as if implying that he should have a dishonorable and heartless attitude toward both his deceased father and his loved ones. But Jesus wasn't saying that the would-be disciple's family was physically dead. Rather, this disciple didn't understand that following Jesus must be life's first and foremost priority. Nothing and no one should stop us from taking the gospel to dying sinners. Loving the Son of God and doing His will should take precedence over everything in life: "If anyone does not love the Lord Jesus Christ, let him be accursed. O Lord, come!" (1 Cor. 16:22).

The Amplified Bible explains the underlying intent of the disciple's words in Matthew 8:21: "Lord, let me first go and bury my father (collect my inheritance)." That puts things into a different light, doesn't it? You don't need any earthly inheritance to follow Christ.

Charles Spurgeon said:

> But with regard to what this man said about burying his father, if there were some force in it to our ear, the Savior who knew everything saw that *there was no force in it*, for He said, "There are other people to bury your father, but I have called upon you now to come and follow me. Nobody else can do that for you, but the burial of your father can be done by others whom I have never called, and who know nothing about the divine life. Let the dead bury their dead."

And then Spurgeon continued:

> You would be surprised if I were to read you the letters which I receive about different things which the writers say I ought to do

170

and could do. Of course, I ought to take a side in politics, and appear at the next political meeting. Of course, I shall not, because there are plenty of dead people to bury dead politics, and they may go and do it. My business is to preach the Gospel. Someone then says, "You should take up social questions." There are plenty of dead people to handle social questions, let them handle them if they like the work, my business is to preach the Gospel of Jesus Christ.

Then it is said, "You ought to provide amusements for the people." Ought I? There are plenty of fools to do that without my going into competition with them, my business is to preach the Gospel. When a man is once called by Christ, he may say of a great many things, "Well, they are very proper, very proper, indeed, for others to attend to. Dead people want burying, and ought to be buried. It is a pity that there should be any difficulty about their being buried, but there are enough dead people to bury them. There are not enough living ones to preach the Gospel, there are not enough to follow Christ." "Follow me," said Christ, "I must be first, and as for these other things, there are other people who can properly attend to them. It is more in their line. The dead know where the graves are, the dead know all about funerals. Follow me, and let the dead bury their dead."[6]

These thoughts from Spurgeon are in line with another hard saying of Jesus: "If anyone comes to Me and does not hate his father and mother, wife and children, brothers and sisters, yes, and his own life also, he cannot be My disciple" (Luke 14:26).

Wait a minute, hate our parents? What about the fifth commandment? If Jesus was saying that we are to detest our parents, spouses, and offspring, it flies directly in the face of the many admonitions that speak of the importance of honoring parents and loving our family. First Timothy 5:8 says, "But if anyone does not provide for his own, and especially for those of his household, he has denied the faith and is worse than an unbeliever."

Rather, Jesus's words in the Gospel of Luke are an example of *hyperbole*, a justified exaggeration to make an important point.

171

Our love for our loved ones and our lives should seem like hatred compared to the love that we have for the God who gave us those loved ones and this life. God is the giver, and all these things are gifts.

The Deadly Cactus

While the Sermon on the Mount is considered by many to contain wonderful truths by which we should live, it's not something to which we want to snuggle up. The Sermon on the Mount is definitely *good* and not *nice*. It is more like a deadly cactus. It shows us how far we fall short of the perfect points of the law. Look closely at Paul's experience:

> But when the commandment came, sin revived and I died. And the commandment, which *was* to *bring* life, I found to *bring* death. (Rom. 7:9–10)

Paul snuggled up to the Law, hoping that it would give him life, but its deadly pricks brought him the opposite. The Law only gives us life if we perfectly fulfill its requirements. Violate them and we die: "The soul who sins shall die" (Ezek. 18:20). In the sermon, Jesus explains God's demands. Rather than comfort us in our sins, the cactus should make us aware of our painful plight.

The Golden Rule and the story of the good Samaritan are indictments of the best of us. Who has always treated others as they would like to be treated, or loved our neighbor as much as we love ourselves? Rather, we are selfish, self-indulgent, sin-loving sinners. Until we understand that, we won't see our sin for what it is—exceedingly sinful. And that means we will never truly seek God's mercy.

Look at the sharp spikes on this cactus:

> You have heard that it was said to those of old, "You shall not commit adultery." But I say to you that whoever looks at a woman to

lust for her has already committed adultery with her in his heart. If your right eye causes you to sin, pluck it out and cast it from you; for it is more profitable for you that one of your members perish, than for your whole body to be cast into hell. And if your right hand causes you to sin, cut it off and cast it from you; for it is more profitable for you that one of your members perish, than for your whole body to be cast into hell. (Matt. 5:27–30)

Do those verses make you feel afraid? They should! Jesus was warning that God requires "truth in the inward parts" (Ps. 51:6). He sees the thought life and the intent, and that knowledge should put the fear of God in us. And it's the fear of the Lord that causes us to depart from evil (see Prov. 16:6). Because lust gives such pleasure to the sinful heart, it causes us to want to desperately protest His words. Surely Jesus isn't saying that looking with sexual desire is morally wrong. There must be some sort of mistake or at least a concession. And so some do protest that because Jesus used the word *adultery* and not *fornication*, perhaps He was only talking about lusting after *married* women.

Let's think about this. If Jesus was forbidding looking with lust at those who are married, a man who wants to have lustful thoughts about a woman should therefore make sure she's single. Should he then approach a prospect and ask if she's single or married? If she is married, he can't lust after her, but if she's single, he can go ahead and indulge in sexually explicit thoughts. Those who are tempted to fall into such an error need to carefully read the words of Jesus again. This is a life-or-death, Heaven-or-hell issue.

One of the most despised methods of the Christian church is the use of fear. That's understandable because many tyrants have used fear to keep the population in control, and certain religions use fear to control people too. However, Jesus used fear legitimately. He said, "My friends, do not be afraid of those who kill the body, and after that have no more that they can do. But I will show you whom you should fear: Fear Him who, after He has killed, has power to cast into hell; yes, I say to you, fear Him!" (Luke 12:4–5).

God doesn't want to control us—if He did, He would never have given us free will. But He does want us to fear Him. Why? Because our fear of God shows that we're in touch with reality. God *should* be feared.

Shark Attacks

The hard sayings of Jesus are important because they keep us on the straight and narrow, away from the detours. We know where we cannot go. Have you ever been enjoying the ocean when the thought of a shark attack crossed your mind? Here's the good news: experts tell us that the chances of getting attacked by a shark are extremely low—one in almost four million.[7] If there is only one chance in four million that I will be attacked, I need not have any real concern as I swim.

But that fear should come back once I know where that statistic comes from. That statistic includes people who are on dry land. The odds change radically when I swim in the ocean. Five people were bitten by sharks at the same Florida beach over one nine-day period in 2019.[8] Therefore, if we absolutely don't want to end up in a shark's stomach, we should stay out of the ocean. That solves the shark attack problem. No sharks on land! And if I don't want death to swallow me, I should stay out of the waters of sin. And the sure way to stay away from sin is to remain on the dry land of the fear of God.

Witnessing Encounter

This conversation took place on a park bench not too far from my house. Joseph was in his late twenties, sincere, and very likable.

However, his opening remarks were both disgusting and blasphemous, but their shock value was wasted because Scripture tells me that every human heart is in a state of enmity toward God (see Rom. 8:7).

RAY: Do you think there's an afterlife?

JOSEPH: Well, there's got to be something right?

RAY: You think about it?

JOSEPH: More than I'd like to, yes. I'm still skeptical. I'm still stubborn about it, but . . .

RAY: Skeptical about what?

JOSEPH: That there is an afterlife.

RAY: You went to a Christian school or a Christian church or something?

JOSEPH: [laughs] I've been kicked out of plenty of them.

RAY: Do you believe in God's existence?

JOSEPH: I'm aware of [expletive]. . . . Sorry for my language.

RAY: You're aware of . . .

JOSEPH: [expletive] existence. I apologize for my language about Him.

RAY: No, that's normal. I'll tell you why; it's because the Bible says the carnal mind—that is, the sinful mind—is in a state of hostility toward God. That's why His name is used as a cuss word. We hate God, the Bible says, for no cause, and the reason we hate Him is the same reason criminals hate the police. It's a moral argument. We don't want God telling us what to do because we love to do that which is wrong. I mean fornication and pornography and stealing; all those things are exciting, and God comes down and says they're a no-no, and we hate Him for that.

JOSEPH: Do we know that's a no-no? We're going off of a word [the Bible] that's been diluted. God hasn't come down here recently and stated the rules. You don't really hear much about Him now in the sense of Him being out here, laying down His wrath, His will, His, you know, commandments, whatever you want to call it. It's like He's not existent almost, and we have to go off of faith, you know, malarkey signs.

RAY: Can I just stop there and say there's so much evidence for God's existence? You're like a fish in the ocean saying, "Where's the ocean? Where's the ocean?" Let me just give you some evidences of God's existence: flowers, birds, trees, sun, moon, stars, seasons, fruits, the human eye, babies, puppies, kittens, ponies; everything you see around you cannot be created by man. We don't know how to make a grain of sand from nothing. The Bible says that the invisible things of God from the creation of the world are clearly seen, and, Joseph, God gave you a conscience— you know right from wrong. The word *conscience* means "with knowledge." *With knowledge.* Every time we do something wrong, we do it with the knowledge that it's wrong. Before, I said that you're in a state of enmity against God, like He's your enemy.

JOSEPH: I wouldn't say that.

RAY: Well, the language you used before is a bit of a clue. Have you ever used God's name as a cuss word?

JOSEPH: A couple of times, yes.

RAY: Have you lied and stolen?

JOSEPH: Of course I have.

RAY: Remember, Jesus said that if you look at a woman with lust, you've committed adultery with her in your heart. Have you ever looked at a woman with lust?

JOSEPH: Of course I have; who hasn't?

RAY: Some homosexuals haven't. So, Joseph, I'm not judging you, but you just told me you're a lying thief, a blasphemer, and an adulterer at heart, and you're like Adam who was running from God because of his sin, trying to hide from God. We're all like that. I was like that before I was a Christian. I was in the car once coming back from a surfing trip, and a bumper sticker on the car in front of me said "God first." That made me so upset, I couldn't wait to get past it. It made me feel weird because I knew God should be first in my life because He gave me life. Everything you've got comes from God: your hearing, your eyesight, your apparatus that you use to fornicate—all come from God. Your teeth, your tongue, your blood, your bones—everything you have is a gift from Him, and you've used His name as a cuss word. There's no thanksgiving in your heart. And so, if God judges you by the Ten Commandments on judgment day, are you going to be innocent or guilty? You'd be guilty on judgment day, and you'd end up in hell—and that grieves me. We've just met, I like you, and the thought of you ending up in hell horrifies me. You may not be concerned, but I am deeply concerned because I know this is deadly serious stuff. Death is the arresting officer that's going to drag you before the judge of the universe, whose law you've violated, and hell is God's prison without parole. And that's terrifying. Now, do you know what God did for guilty sinners so we wouldn't have to go to hell? Sounds like you had a Christian background; tell me, what did God do so you wouldn't have to—

JOSEPH: Died for our sins, so you know, right? He died for all our sins.

RAY: You and I broke God's law; Jesus paid the fine. Just before He died, He said something weird. He said three words: "It is finished." In other words, the debt has been paid. If you're in court and someone pays the fine, the judge can let you go. He can show you mercy, and justice can be done. When Jesus suffered and died on the cross and cried "It is finished," He was saying that debt is paid. That means God can legally commute your death sentence. He can let you live forever. He can forgive your sins—let you walk out of the courtroom—all because of the death and resurrection of the Savior. What you have to do is repent and trust in Him. I trust today you've seen the seriousness of sin in a new light, that your lust is adultery, hatred is murder, and lying lips are an abomination to the Lord . . . that the death sentence comes from sinning against God. He takes it seriously, and because it's so serious you might be able to find a place of sorrow in your heart for sin, to realize that Jesus suffered and died on the cross to take the punishment in your stead so you could live forever. That's what happened on that cross and it should break your heart. Man, if I took a bullet for you, wouldn't you kind of respect me and not use my name as a cuss word? You'd say, "Man, you did that for me?"

JOSEPH: What you're saying is on point. The thing is, *He* took the rap, not His Father.

RAY: The Bible says, "God was in Christ reconciling the world to Himself."[9] *God was in Christ.* The Old Testament says, "A body You have prepared for Me."[10] Jesus Christ was the express image of the invisible God.

JOSEPH: But in a physical form, right?

RAY: Yes, in a physical form.

JOSEPH: Born of the womb.

RAY: You're not going to die if you haven't got a body, so God had to create a body to suffer because He is spirit, and that's what happened on that cross. So, man, please think about this, think about your sins, think about the Savior, think about the prodigal son. Remember what brought him back to his father? He realized he was desiring pig food. That brought him to his senses. And if you search your heart, the desires of your heart would be for filth. So it should bring you to your senses, to say, "Lord, I've sinned against You; please forgive me," and He will. What were you going to say?

JOSEPH: Please forgive me?

RAY: That's what you need to say to God. Just go vertical with your repentance. God will change your heart and give you a love for righteousness, which is a miracle for sin-loving sinners. Listen, I care about you. I love you and I don't want you to end up in hell.

JOSEPH: It would be my fate.

RAY: So would you please think about this?

JOSEPH: Sure.

RAY: It's not your fate. You're wearing a devil's T-shirt; you're serving the devil at the moment. Satan is your master, and his will you do. So it's not your fate. Come to God, and say, "God, forgive me," and He'll change you. Come out of a kingdom of darkness into light. So are you going to think about what we talked about?

JOSEPH: Of course I will.

RAY: Ok. Thanks for talking to me, man; I really appreciate it.

JOSEPH: No problem.

He didn't need any nice words from me—I mean, I encouraged him, of course, and thanked him for his time. But we can be like Jesus and use the hard sayings when we need to use them. Sinners aren't going to stay out of hell because someone told them that fornicating, lying, and blaspheming are all right and that God won't care. Bring them before the law of God and give them the truth, even when it's difficult to say. Be the sign that points toward Jesus because sinners will take any chance at a detour away from Him.

12 | Jesus and His Demand for Love

God created us from nothing. Such a thought is mind-boggling because we can only create nothing from nothing. We *need* something to create something. We need the raw materials to make an omelet. It wasn't too long ago that we were nothing ourselves. We didn't exist. But God used our parents to freely give us life. And then He further lavished His kindness upon us with the beauty of creation—the breathtaking blue skies, colorful birds, tall trees, luscious fruits, vibrant colors, and music to give us pleasure as well as love and laughter. But the kindness and the great love God has for us were gathered together as one brilliant beam of sunlight "through the tender mercy of our God, with which the Dayspring from on high has visited us; to give light to those who sit in darkness and the shadow of death" (Luke 1:78–79).

It was the ultimate act of kindness—the unspeakable gift of the cross: "But God clearly shows and proves His own love for us, by the fact that while we were still sinners, Christ died for us" (Rom. 5:8 AMP).

What does He then require in return for such love? This: "'You shall love the Lord your God with all your heart, with all your soul, and with all your mind.' This is the first and great commandment. And the second is like it: 'You shall love your neighbor as yourself.' On these two commandments hang all the Law and the Prophets" (Matt. 22:37–40).

After such evident displays of love, we should have no problem loving God. But we sometimes do. We make something simple into something very complex. I received the following email from a distraught young lady:

> I've been "saved" for around 4 years, I have a strong belief in God. I fully believe what Jesus did on the cross and understand the legal transaction as explained in your videos. When I was first saved, I was on fire; nothing could stop me talking about God. Then very very slowly I slid back into the world. My beliefs about God never changed. I just ignored them. I started smoking again and now unfortunately I'm having great difficulty stopping. My question is HOW do I get that fire for God back?! I pray daily, I've repented but I can't kick the smoking habit as much as I need to. I watch your videos every day to examine myself against the commandments and I also read the Bible daily, albeit not a great amount maybe just a verse or other days a chapter or two, but I do read it daily. How do I get my relationship back with God and become truly born again? I don't think about much else—it's so important but I don't know how to obtain it. Please help!

My answer to her, and to any of you who are thinking the same thing, goes like this: There was a certain husband and wife who, for the first few years of marriage, loved each other with a passion. But over time, the husband slowly lost both his love and his concern for his wife. He became more involved in his work and sports, and those things eventually became his passion.

Because of this, he stopped buying her gifts and showing her those little acts of love that happened in the first few years of marriage. As time further passed, he began to consider getting a divorce. This was a great tragedy because his faithful wife never wavered in her love for him. She daily prepared his meals, washed his clothes, and catered to his every need.

During their early years of marriage, she showed how much she loved him. He had contracted a serious lung disease brought on by his heavy smoking. The doctors said that the cancer would kill him if he didn't find a lung donor. She proved to be a perfect match, and at great physical pain to herself, she gave up a portion of one of her lungs for him. That sacrifice saved his life, but it left her with such shortness of breath that she was permanently confined to a respirator and a wheelchair. Yet with all the suffering, she never regretted her sacrifice. Such was her love for her beloved spouse.

If the husband came to you to get advice on whether he should begin divorce proceedings, what would you say to him? Hopefully, you would look him in the eye and tell him that he is a hard-hearted wretch of a man. His next best step would be to get on his knees in front of his dear, sweet wife and plead for her forgiveness. You would perhaps then explain that his love for her is a choice. In light of her sacrifice, it should be a joy to return her love. His love may feel dutiful at first, but as he shows her acts of kindness, tender feelings should follow because they will be ignited by gratitude for her sacrifice.

I'm sure you see how it relates. What should we feel in the light of the sacrifice of the cross? Maybe sometimes you "feel" nothing. Don't let that deceive you. Are you perhaps considering divorcing yourself from Jesus and going back to the world? If so, you should fall on your knees for such a terrible sin and plead with God for His forgiveness: "Adulterers and adulteresses! Do you not know that friendship with the world is enmity with God? Whoever therefore wants to be a friend of the world makes himself an enemy of God" (James 4:4).

Any fleeting thoughts of falling away can enter our minds only if there is a shallow knowledge of the nature of sin. That leaves us with a lack of understanding of what happened at the cross, and the result is a lack of genuine repentance. And if there's no repentance, we are unsaved, despite a profession of faith.

There is a popular American reality-television series that debuted on March 11, 2012, on the Animal Planet channel. The series follows members of the Fish and Game Department as they track down those who are violating the law among other things.

In one program, an officer approached two women and one man in their early twenties. The male had a fishing license; however, the two females who had been fishing didn't. One began posing for the camera, obviously flippant about not having a license. As the officer was writing the ticket, he looked at the camera and said that to her not having a license was nothing but a joke. He then said to watch her demeanor change when she saw the $94 ticket. And it certainly did. The cost of the ticket showed her that fishing without a license was a serious offense.

Sinners think that sin is a big joke *until they understand the fine that has to be paid.* The fine is death and damnation. But even the threat of hell is a big joke until the law connects with the conscience. The conscience then springs to life and accuses of sin—the intuitive knowledge of right and wrong gives credibility to the Ten Commandments. When that happens, suddenly sin is seen as deadly serious. That produces fear, and that legitimate fear of danger prepares the human heart for the mercy of the cross. That fear is lacking in the hearts of many. To remedy the problem, we should earnestly pray for a revelation of God's holiness and of our absolute sinfulness, and then we should meditate on the cost of the cross.

If that doesn't break our hearts and produce both the fear of God and the fuel of gratitude, we should show our love anyway by doing what we know pleases Him. In time, the feelings will follow. How could I not simply present myself as a living sacrifice in the light of such love? As it says in Romans, "I beseech you therefore, brethren, by the mercies of God, that you present your bodies a living sacrifice, holy, acceptable to God, which is your reasonable service. And do not be conformed to this world, but be transformed by the renewing of your mind, that you may prove what is that good and acceptable and perfect will of God" (12:1–2).

The key to my having a vibrant relationship with God is to yield my heart and soul to Him. That's my "reasonable service." In other words, it's the right thing to do. That husband should joyfully serve his beloved wife in the light of her sacrifice—because it is the right thing for him to do, whether or not he feels like it.

|||||||||||||

It was a big moment when someone had the bright idea to invert the ketchup bottle. For many years, millions of Americans would pick up a bottle at a diner to put the finishing touch on what sat on their plate. Then they would spend the next few moments frustratingly holding the bottle upside down with one hand and pounding it on the bottom with the other hand. If that didn't work, they would resort to sticking a knife into the bottle to try and dislodge the ketchup. This resulted in a messy knife, coated in red goop up to the handle. More often than not, it also sent a flying burst of ketchup that could hit those at the next table. It was a predictable, messy, and annoying procedure. At one point, Heinz tried to give this negative a positive spin. Back in 1978, they ran a series of television advertisements trying to convince hungry sauce seekers that it was worth the bottle battle by using Carly Simon's famous song "Anticipation" as background music.

Then came wonderful relief in 2002. Someone invented the inverted wide-mouthed bottle. By widening the lid and inverting the label, the lid became the bottom, and gravity kicked in and did the rest. The substance now sat at the mouth of the container and readily poured out on the waiting food with little effort. It was a simple but brilliant marketing step that solved an age-old customer frustration, and much to the delight of Heinz, people used more ketchup: "Within a year of introducing the inverted bottle, Heinz was growing three times as quickly as its competition. In a sleepy market, that's a big win. In the ensuing years, their ketchup sales grew at 25% per year, most of that growth taken from competitors."[1]

For many years, there has been a worrying lack of evangelistic flow. Frustratingly few reach out to the lost. Despite the pounding of pulpits, few in the pews pour out their lives into this unsaved world. But when we have a personal Gethsemane experience, we are turned upside down. When we earnestly pray, "Not my will, but Yours be done," everything changes. Then, spreading the gospel becomes a delight—because we know we are doing God's will. Evangelism becomes a natural outpouring of the love of God that has been shed abroad in their hearts. And that, any evangelist will tell you, is the source of our joy.

In this chapter, I've used two analogies regarding evangelistic zeal. The first was to liken it to a good marriage in which love and sacrifice are practiced, even when feelings are absent. The second was to compare it to the widened upside-down mouth of the ketchup bottle. Here is the same lesson using a third analogy.

I didn't sleep too well one night because I had a lot of script to memorize for a video shoot. The reason I was having trouble sleeping was my concern that I wouldn't get enough sleep. However, after some time I was able to drift off.

When I got up in the morning, I had a lot to keep in mind. I had to print out the script so that I would have bullet points. I had to remember to take Sam's sunglasses in case the director wanted him in the shot, and I would need a stake to push into the ground for his leash if he wasn't in the shot. I needed copies of my book and a black shirt to hide the clip-on microphone. Finally, I got in my car and drove to work, pleased with myself that I remembered all these essentials. As I neared the ministry building, I noticed that my feet felt warm, even though it was a cold morning. And they weren't just warm, they were too warm. I was still wearing my slippers!

Sometimes we are so busy with other things that we forget to make sure we are wearing the right shoes—and I'm not talking about slippers and loafers. I'm talking about our gospel shoes. These aren't simply shoes; they are an attitude: "Having shod your feet with the preparation of the gospel of peace" (Eph. 6:15). When we want to do something, we make plans to do it. We prepare. Whether it's buying something, meeting someone, or just fixing a meal, it begins in the mind with a plan of preparation. The word *preparation* means "the action or process of making ready or being made ready for use or consideration."[2] Here is Ephesians 6:15 in the Amplified Bible: "Having strapped on your feet the gospel of peace in preparation [to face the enemy with firm-footed stability and the readiness produced by the good news]."

Slippers are for indoors. Shoes are designed for hard surfaces. Our souls must be firm. That means we need a resolute attitude. I say to myself, *Today, reaching the lost has priority. Writing books, editing, filming, food, entertainment—everything else I do takes a back seat. I will not waste the precious day by ignoring the unsaved.* But one day, I almost did. It was tantamount to taking a detour myself!

Witnessing Encounter

It was early on a Sunday morning in the middle of November during the 2020 pandemic. Our staff had been restricted from coming to work, and I had to help with packing boxes and doing a few other odd jobs at the ministry. One of those odd jobs was regularly cleaning up a week's worth of trash that was left in the alley next to our building. It was a job I dreaded not because it was a lowly task but because some of the things I would have to handle turned my stomach. People had no conscience about what they left for others to pick up.

On this Sunday morning, I saw a figure walking toward me, talking to himself. I became a little nervous as he drew closer. He was wearing black along with a black facial mask. I was alone in the alley and felt rather vulnerable. I looked at the broom in my hand and thought that it would be the only means of self-defense if he attacked me. At the best of times, I'm not excited to witness to the lost. In fact, I never have any joy when I'm about to share the gospel. Rather, I have a measure of controlled fear. But I never fail to bubble with joy afterward, knowing that I had been true and faithful to both God and man. I always drag my feet going and click my heels coming back.

As the scary man drew closer, I said a friendly, "Good morning." He responded by saying he was going to help me. His "help" was simply to pick up old cigarette butts and marijuana stubs so that he could smoke them. As I swept the trash into piles, I began thinking that I was hard-hearted. I didn't feel any concern for this man's salvation. All I was concerned about was my own safety. I try to be wise when it comes to putting myself into vulnerable situations, and I felt that this had the potential to be dangerous. Still, I felt a sense of guilt because I really didn't want to witness to him when I always do with others.

As I was having these thoughts, he suddenly said, "Have you talked to God today?" I was surprised and said that I had. I also took that as a prompting to share the gospel, despite my suspicion that he was demonically possessed. I learned that his name was Tony, and when I asked him if he thought he was a good person, he responded that he was. However, when I took him through the Ten Commandments, he began trying to justify himself by saying he had only stolen when he was younger. He said he had never blasphemed, nor had he lusted after women. But he conceded that he was guilty of looking at pornography. He then became a little angry and accused me of judging him. I told him that I wasn't judging him but was trying to show him that he needed God's mercy. Then I quickly shared the cross, the resurrection, and the necessity of repenting and trusting in Jesus for his salvation.

After he left, I felt pleased to still be alive but ashamed that I was slow to let my little light shine. I determined that the next time I would be a little quicker.

Final Word

I hope this book has been helpful to you. If you began reading it unsure of where you will spend eternity, I earnestly pray that you've resolved the issue of your eternal salvation—that you've seen that the gospel is the only way to God. The gospel tells us how to avoid hell and instead to attain Heaven. And there's nothing on earth as important as this. Everything else besides the gospel of Christ is a detour that leads to only one place.

In closing, let me talk about something with which I'm sure you can relate. Most of us have had to deal with passwords. A generation or so ago we didn't lock our cars, set security alarms, or have to sign ridiculously long contracts when buying a car. We would hand over the cash, be given the owner's papers, shake a hand, and the car became ours. But as sin has become more prevalent, trust has disappeared and been replaced by locks, alarms, contracts, and annoying passwords.

The reason passwords are annoying is because they have to be changed regularly and are therefore easily forgotten. And that is frustrating. However, any frustration you and I have had with forgotten passwords is dwarfed by one man who forgot his:

The San Francisco man who can't remember the password to unlock his $220 million Bitcoin fortune says he long ago "made peace" with the reality he may never gain access. Stefan Thomas went viral this week after a New York Times profile revealed to the world his unsettling dilemma: The password to unlock his Bitcoin fortune is locked in a hard drive that gives users 10 attempts before wiping clean. Thomas has just two more tries.[1]

In an interview, he said that it had been a long nine years since he first realized he'd been locked out of his account. That gave him plenty of time to process it. He said, "There were sort of a couple weeks where I was just desperate, I don't have any other word to describe it." He added, "You sort of question your own self-worth. What kind of person loses something that important?"[2]

The frustration is that the password is sitting somewhere in his memory bank; he just can't recall it. If he could, he would instantly have $220 million. He had ten chances to recall it—eight have already failed.

But his loss is *nothing* compared to the riches that sinners will miss out on because they don't know the "password" for their salvation. Most wrongly think that by keeping the Ten Commandments they will get a free pass into Heaven. But none of the ten will let them in: "The commandment, which was to bring life, I found to bring death" (Rom. 7:10).

Why would anyone follow Jesus? Because God's grace in Christ unlocks the doors of immortality, saves us from wrath, and gives us treasure in earthen vessels.

May God bless you and use you to point others to the grace that is only in Jesus. He is the only way to Heaven. Everything else is merely a detour away from Him. Jesus alone is the way, the truth, and the life.

Notes

Chapter 1 Jesus and Intellectual Arguments

1. Owen Jarus, "Who Was Jesus?," Live Science, August 2, 2019, https://www.livescience.com/3482-jesus-man.html.

2. Christopher Klein, "The Bible Says Jesus Was Real. What Other Proof Exists?," History, updated March 24, 2021, https://www.history.com/news/was-jesus-real-historical-evidence.

3. Klein, "The Bible Says Jesus Was Real."

4. Hosea 4:6.

5. Psalm 111:10.

6. Hebrews 10:31.

7. See Matthew 10:28.

8. See Matthew 10:28.

9. Proverbs 16:6 KJV.

10. Proverbs 12:22.

11. Romans 6:23.

12. 2 Corinthians 7:10.

13. Available at LivingWaters.com.

Chapter 2 Jesus and Hope

1. Rob Walker, "Don McClean on the Tragedy behind American Pie: 'I Cried for Two Years,'" *Guardian*, October 22, 2020, https://apple.news/AjINvwK7SSR6DdK_a-EBXIw.

2. Wikipedia, s.v. "All work and no play makes Jack a dull boy," last edited June 11, 2021, https://en.wikipedia.org/wiki/All_work_and_no_play_makes_Jack_a_dull_boy.

3. Elizabeth Hlavinka, "CDC Details COVID-19's Massive Mental Health Impact," MedPage Today, August 14, 2020, https://www.medpagetoday.com/psychiatry/generalpsychiatry/88074.

4. See John 14:21.

Chapter 3 Jesus and Money

1. John Wesley, "John Wesley's Bible Commentary Notes—Matthew 8," Bible Explore, accessed August 12, 2021, http://www.godrules.net/library/wesley/wesleymat8.htm.

Chapter 4 Jesus and Exclusivity

1. David Sørensen, "What Is the Right Translation of John 14:6 from Greek to English?," Quora, accessed July 12, 2021, https://www.quora.com/What-is-the-right-translation-of-John-14-6-from-Greek-to-English.
2. "Falls," World Health Organization, April 26, 2021, https://www.who.int/news-room/fact-sheets/detail/falls.
3. Ashish Tiwari, "Skydiving: How Fast Can You Fall through the Air?," Science ABC, updated September 9, 2020, https://www.scienceabc.com/eyeopeners/skydiving-how-fast-can-you-fall-through-the-air-terminal-velocity.html.
4. Luke 23:43.
5. Ephesians 2:8–9.
6. John 14:6.

Chapter 5 Jesus and the Crazy World

1. Randall Buth, "That Small-Fry Herod Antipas, or When a Fox Is Not a Fox," Jerusalem Perspective, September 1, 1993, https://www.jerusalemperspective.com/2667/.
2. "Who was Herodias in the Bible?," Got Questions, accessed June 30, 2021, https://www.gotquestions.org/Herodias-in-the-Bible.html.
3. Leda Reynolds, "Arkansas Man Shoots Woman Dead over Botched Fast Food Order, Police Say," *Newsweek*, October 2, 2020, https://apple.news/A55o7VnWJS_C_xqFxFPkgpQ.
4. Acts 28:23.
5. See 2 Timothy 3:1.
6. Owen Jarus, "Ancient Israel: A Brief History," *Live Science*, August 15, 2016, https://www.livescience.com/55774-ancient-israel.html.
7. John 7:7.
8. Matthew 5:28.
9. John 3:16.

Chapter 6 Jesus and Authority

1. Marissa Wenzke, Chris Wolfe, "Video Shows Two Deputies Ambushed, Shot While Inside Patrol Vehicle in Compton; Gunman at Large: LASD," KTLA5, September 12, 2020, https://ktla.com/news/local-news/l-a-county-sheriffs-deputy-shot-in-compton-agency-says/.
2. Samuel Chadwick, LibQuotes, accessed August 12, 2021, https://libquotes.com/samuel-chadwick/quote/lbt7b1x.
3. "Matthew Henry's Bible Commentary (concise): Commentary on Acts 3:12–18," Christianity.com, accessed July 1, 2021, https://www.christianity.com/bible/commentary.php?com=mhc&b=44&c=3.

4. "Mens Rea," Cornell Law School, accessed July 1, 2021, https://www.law
.cornell.edu/wex/mens_rea.
5. Proverbs 28:26.
6. Romans 6:23.

Chapter 7 Jesus and His Accusers

1. See Deuteronomy 5:16.
2. Matthew 5:28.
3. Exodus 20:3.
4. See Romans 5:8 KJV.

Chapter 8 Jesus and the Greatest Sermon

1. Augustus Toplady, "Rock of Ages," 1763, public domain.
2. Charles Spurgeon, "The First Beatitude," August 5, 1909, Christian Clas-
sics Ethereal Library, https://www.ccel.org/ccel/spurgeon/sermons55.xxxii.html.
3. 1 Corinthians 15:55.
4. Romans 6:23.
5. John 19:30.
6. John Newton, "Amazing Grace," 1772, public domain.

Chapter 9 Jesus and the Lost

1. This principle is expanded in a teaching that can be freely heard on the
bottom of the homepage of our website, LivingWaters.com. Many times those
who have listened to it said they didn't get it until they listened twice.
2. John Bunyan, *The Pilgrim's Progress* (London) 1815, public domain.

Chapter 10 Jesus and Atheism

1. Machine Philosophy, "Sam Harris v William Lane Craig Debate: 'Is the
Foundation of Morality Natural or Supernatural?,'" MandM, May 3, 2011, http://
www.mandm.org.nz/2011/05/transcript-sam-harris-v-william-lane-craig-debate
-"is-good-from-god".html.
2. Agatan Foundation, "Best of Non Believers Arguments and Comebacks
Part 2," YouTube video, 30:09, posted by "Agatan Foundation," October 9, 2015,
https://youtu.be/eBBoGAHCJ-8.
3. Online Etymology Dictionary, s.v. "cosmos," accessed July 7, 2021, https://
www.etymonline.com/word/cosmos.
4. "Just," Lexico, accessed August 30, 2021, https://www.lexico.com/en
/definition/just.
5. Machine Philosophy, "Sam Harris v William Lane Craig Debate."
6. Toplady, "Rock of Ages."
7. Sam Harris, *Letter to a Christian Nation* (New York: Vintage Books, 2008), 25.
8. "Isaac Newton," Goodreads, accessed August 30, 2021, https://www
.goodreads.com/quotes/10151203-atheism-is-so-senseless-when-i-look-at-the
-solar.

9. Matthew 5:28.
10. Genesis 38:7.
11. See Luke 12:20.

Chapter 11 Jesus and His Hard Sayings

1. Walter Isaacson, "Einstein and Faith," *Time*, April 5, 2007, http://content
.time.com/time/subscriber/article/0,33009,1607298,00.html.
2. Josh McDowell, *Evidence that Demands a Verdict: Fast Answers for Skeptics' Questions* (Nashville: Thomas Nelson, 1999), EPUB.
3. Lu Paradise, "What Famous and Infamous People Had to Say About Jesus," Paradise Post Blog, August 25, 2010, https://paradisepostblog.wordpress.com
/what-famous-infamous-people-had-to-say-about-jesus/.
4. Jeff Fountain, "Destined for Eternity," ArtWay, October 30, 2011, https://
www.artway.eu/content.php?id=1042&action=show&lang=en.
5. Thomas Jefferson, "From Thomas Jefferson to Benjamin Waterhouse, 26 June 1822," *Founders Online*, National Archives, accessed August 12, 2021, https://
founders.archives.gov/documents/Jefferson/98-01-02-2905.
6. C. H. Spurgeon, "Fickle Followers," September 11, 1892, Spurgeon Gems, accessed July 9, 2021, emphasis original, https://www.spurgeongems.org/sermon
/chs2273.pdf.
7. Aylin Woodward, "5 People Were Bitten by Sharks at the Same Florida Beach over 9 Days," *Business Insider*, August 6, 2019, https://www.businessinsider.com
/florida-shark-attack-expert-tips-how-to-avoid-2019-7.
8. Woodward, "5 People Were Bitten by Sharks."
9. 2 Corinthians 5:19.
10. Hebrews 10:5.

Chapter 12 Jesus and His Demand for Love

1. Frank Greve, "Ketchup Is Better with Upside-Down, Bigger Bottle," *McClatchy*, updated June 28, 2007, https://www.mcclatchydc.com/news/nation
-world/national/article24465613.html.
2. "Prepare," Lexico, accessed August 30, 2021, https://www.lexico.com/en
/definition/preparation.

Final Word

1. Liz Kreutz, "SF Man Who Can't Remember Bitcoin Password Says He's 'Made Peace' with $220M loss," ABC 7 News, January 14, 2021, https://abc7news
.com/stefan-thomas-bitcoin-password-san-francisco/9635218.
2. Kreutz, "SF Man Who Can't Remember Bitcoin Password."

Ray Comfort is an experienced apologist and popular speaker who has written over one hundred books, including *Faith Is for Weak People* and *Anyone but Me*. Cohost of the award-winning TV program *Way of the Master*, which airs across the globe, Comfort is the executive producer of several award-winning movies that have been seen by millions (www.fullyfreefilms.com). He and his wife, Sue, live in Southern California.

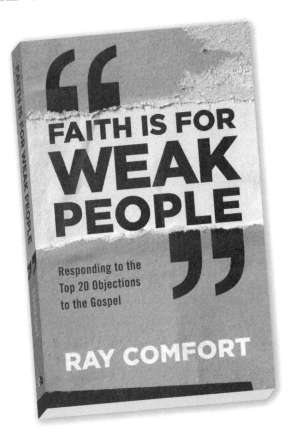

Isaiah said, "HERE I AM, LORD. SEND ME." We say, "HERE I AM, LORD. SEND ANYONE BUT ME."

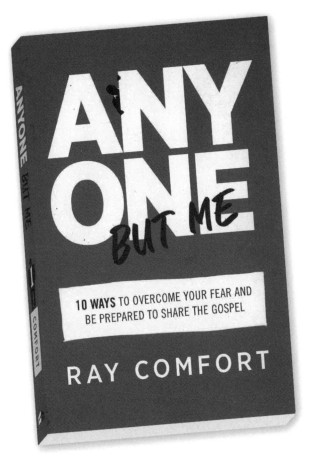

Filmmaker and bestselling author Ray Comfort equips you to confidently and fearlessly share your faith with the unsaved so you will always be ready to "give an answer for the hope that you have," helping lead people to Christ.

KEEP UP WITH
RAY and HIS MINISTRY

LIVING WATERS publishes daily witnessing clips on YouTube (over 175,000,000 views). Watching these will help to equip you to share your faith.

LIVINGWATERS.COM

 @RayComfort // @LivingWatersPub

@Living Waters

@official.Ray.Comfort